Rewriting

Rewriting
How to Do Things with Texts

Joseph Harris

UTAH STATE UNIVERSITY PRESS
Logan, Utah

Utah State University Press
Logan, Utah 84322

Copyright © 2006 Utah State University Press

Printed on acid-free paper

Cover design by Barbara Yale-Read
Manufactured in the United States of America

Library of Congress Cataloging-in-Publication Data

Harris, Joseph (Joseph D.)
Rewriting : how to do things with texts / Joseph Harris.
p. cm.
Includes index.
ISBN 0-87421-642-7 (pbk. : alk. paper)
1. English language--Rhetoric--Study and teaching. 2. Persuasion (Rhetoric)--Study and teaching. 3. Academic writing--Study and teaching. I. Title.
PE1404.H363 2006
808.042071--dc22
2006004631

For Kate and Mora

Contents

Introduction   *1*

1   Coming to Terms   *13*

2   Forwarding   *34*

3   Countering   *54*

4   Taking an Approach   *73*

5   Revising   *98*

Afterword: Teaching Rewriting   *124*

Acknowledgments   *135*

Index   *137*

Introduction

A text is made up of multiple writings, drawn from many cultures and entering into mutual relations of dialogue, parody, contestation.

—Roland Barthes, "The Death of the Author"

My aim in this book is to help you make interesting use of the texts you read in the essays you write. How do you respond to the work of others in a way that is both generous and assertive? How do you make their words and thoughts part of what *you* want to say? In the academy you will often be asked to situate your thoughts about a text or an issue in relation to what others have written about it. Indeed, I'd argue that this interplay of ideas defines academic writing—that whatever else they may do, intellectuals almost always write *in response* to the work of others.

> **Intertexts**
>
> As Jonathan Culler writes: "Literary works are not to be considered autonomous entities, 'organic wholes,' but as intertextual constructs: sequences which have meaning in relation to other texts which they take up, cite, parody, refute, or generally transform." *The Pursuit of Signs* (Ithaca, NY: Cornel University Press, 1981), 38.

1

(Literary theorists call this aspect of writing *intertextuality*.) But to respond is to do more than to recite or ventriloquize; we expect a respondent to add something to what is being talked about. The question for an academic writer, then, is how to come up with this something else, to add to what has already been said.

My advice here is to imagine yourself as *rewriting*—as drawing from, commenting on, adding to—the work of others. Almost all academic essays and books contain within them the visible traces of other texts—in the form of notes, quotations, citations, charts, figures, illustrations, and the like. This book is about the writing that needs to go on around these traces, about what you need to do to make the work of others an integral part of your own thinking and writing. This kind of work often gets talked about in ways—avoiding plagiarism, documenting sources, citing authorities, acknowledging influences—that make it seem a dreary and legalistic concern. But for me this misses the real excitement of intellectual writing—which is the chance to engage with and rewrite the work of other thinkers. The job of an intellectual is to push at and question what has been said before, to rethink and reinterpret the texts he or she is dealing with. More than anything else, then, I hope in this book to encourage you to take a stance toward the work of others that, while generous and fair, is also playful, questioning, and assertive.

This has led some readers to ask why I've chosen a term like *rewriting* to describe this sort of active and critical stance. And, certainly, I hope it's clear that the kind of rewriting I value has nothing to do with simply copying or reciting the work of others. Quite the contrary. My goal is to show you some ways of *using* their texts for your purposes. The reason I call this *rewriting* is to point to a generative paradox of academic work: Like all writers, intellectuals need to say something new and say it well. But unlike many other writers, what intellectuals have to say is bound up inextricably with the books we are reading, the movies we are watching, the music we are listening to, and the ideas of the people we are talking with. Our creativity thus has its roots in the work of others—in response, reuse, and rewriting.

Rewriting is also a usefully specific and concrete word; it refers not to a feeling or idea but to an action. In this book I approach rewriting as what the ethnographer Sylvia Scribner has called a *social practice:* the use of certain tools (paper, pen, computer) in a well-defined context (the academy) to achieve a certain end or make a particular product (a critical essay). There are practices in all walks of life—ways of farming and gardening, of working with leather

Intertexts

Sylvia Scribner, "The Practice of Literacy," in *Mind and Social Practice* (New York: Cambridge University Press, 1997), 190–205.

or wood, of interviewing clients and counseling patients, of teaching and coaching, of designing and engineering, of setting up labs and conducting experiments. A practice describes how the members of a particular craft or trade get their work done. A problem with many books on writing, it seems to me, is that they fail to imagine their subject in meaningful terms as such a practice. Instead, they tend to alternate between offering advice that is specific but trivial—about proofreading or copyediting, for instance—and exhortations that are as earnest as they are vague. Or at least I have never felt sure that I knew what I was actually being asked to do when called upon to "think critically" or to "take risks" or to "approach revision as re-vision." But by looking here at academic writing as a social practice, as a set of strategies that intellectuals put to use in working with texts, I hope to describe some of its key moves with a useful specificity.

Much of my thinking about writing hinges on this idea of a *move*. My subtitle alludes to one of the quirkiest and most intriguing books I have ever read, the philosopher J. L. Austin's *How to Do Things with Words*. In this book, actually the notes from a series of lectures, Austin argues that in thinking about language his fellow philosophers have long been overconcerned with decoding the precise meaning or truth value of various statements—a fixation that has blinded them from considering the routine yet complex ways in which people use words *to get things done:* to marry, to promise, to bet, to apologize, to persuade, to contract, and the like. Austin calls such uses of language *performatives* and suggests that it is often more useful to ask what a speaker is trying *to do* in saying something than what he or she means by it.

While I don't try to apply Austin's thinking here in any exact way, I do think of myself as working in his mode—as trying to show how to do things with texts, to shift our talk about writing away from the fixed and static language of thesis and structure and toward a more dynamic vocabulary of action, gesture, and response. You *move* in tandem with or in response to others, as part of a game or dance or performance or conversation—sometimes toward a goal and sometimes just to keep the ball in play or the talk going, sometimes to win and sometimes to contribute to the work of a group. I hope in this book to describe intellectual writing as such a fluid and social activity and to offer you some strategies, some moves as a writer, for participating in it.

To do so, I draw on my experiences over the last twenty years as a writer and teacher of academic writing. And so, while this book is filled with examples of intellectuals at work with texts, they are examples that perhaps, in the end, tell as much about my own tastes, training, and values as anything else. That is to say, in this book I use my own ways of responding to and working with texts, my own habits of reading and writing, as representative of what other academics and intellectuals do. The drawback of such an approach, I suspect, is not that it is likely to be idiosyncratic but the reverse—that I may end up simply rehashing the common sense, the accepted practices, of a particular group of writers. But that is also, in a way, my goal: to show you some of the moves that academics routinely make with texts, to articulate part of "what goes without saying" about such work.

The Structure of This Book

Each of the chapters in this book centers on a particular rewriting move: *coming to terms, forwarding, countering, taking an approach,* and *revising.* But these five moves do not by any means compose a fixed sequence for writing a critical essay. On the contrary, I am sure that as you work on different pieces, you will find yourself using these moves in varying ways and for shifting reasons—sometimes making several moves almost at once and other times focusing on a particular use of a text, sometimes making sustained use of a certain move and other times not employing it at all. I have ordered the chapters of this book, however, to suggest a kind of ethics of academic writing, a sense that intellectual work both starts and ends in acknowledging the strengths of other perspectives. And so I begin with what might be called the *generous* aspects of working with texts before turning to more *critical* forms of rewriting.

In chapter 1, I suggest some strategies for *coming to terms* with complex texts, for re-presenting the work of others in ways that are both fair to them and useful to your own aims in writing. In a sense, this is rewriting in its clearest form. For as soon as you begin to say what you think a text is "about" you are involved in rewriting it, in translating its language into your own. But how do you offer the gist of an ambitious, complex, and perhaps quite long text in the space of a few paragraphs or sentences? How do you select certain phrases or ideas for emphasis? When do you quote and when do you paraphrase? For while the point of academic writing is never merely to explain what someone else has said, to respond to others you need also to offer an accurate account of their work, one that respects its strengths as well as notes its limits. Effective use begins in generous understanding.

In chapter 2, I look more closely at such questions of use—specifically, at strategies for *forwarding* the projects of others. I borrow the term *forward* from the language of email because I think it describes better than *respond* what writers most often actually do with other texts. For outside of a few situations (teaching, editing, personal letters), readers seldom respond directly *to* a writer with comments on his or her text ("Dear Mr. Shakespeare . . ."). They are instead more likely to forward their thoughts *about* that text for a group of other readers—the teachers and students in a course, perhaps, or the readers of a journal or magazine or website—much as email users often resend posts that they think will interest certain friends and colleagues, usually with a set of carats (>) or a vertical line marking off the original text from their own comments. Anyone who has participated in a listserv knows how complicated and layered such posts can grow, as members insert remarks and delete passages before reforwarding a post back to the group, often resulting in a palimpsest of comments upon comments upon comments upon an original post. While I don't want to push this analogy too far, I do want to hold onto the idea of academic writing as involving this sort of ongoing recirculation of texts. As I use the term, then, a writer *forwards* the views of another when he or she takes terms and concepts from one text and applies them to a reading of other texts or situations. The most important questions to ask a writer at such points often have less to do with the text being read than with the uses being made of it. In coming to terms with a text, your focus lies on understanding and representing its argument. In forwarding a text, you seek to extend the range and power of its ideas and phrasings. In this sense, the first two chapters sketch out ways of reading *with* an author, of rewriting as building upon the work of others.

Chapter 3 offers a mirror image of this emphasis, suggesting ways of reading *against* the grain of a text, of rewriting as a way of *countering* ideas and phrasings that strike you as somehow mistaken, troubling, or incomplete. I don't explore here the (limited) dynamics of pro-and-con debates, of writing whose aim is to simply to prove why someone else is foolish or wrong. For such work aims not at rewriting but erasure. Instead, I look at some of the ways you can develop what you have to say as a writer by thinking through the limits and problems of other views and texts. Such work involves more than shouting down an opponent or finding ways of discounting her or his arguments; an effective counterstatement must attend closely to the strengths of the position it is responding to, and thus in many ways depends on representing that position clearly and fairly in order to make full sense. The characteristic stance of the counterstatement is " *Yes, but...*". This sort of rewriting—in which a writer aims less to refute or negate than to rethink or qualify—seems to me one of the key moves of intellectual discourse.

Projects

Identifying Writerly Moves

See if you can locate texts that offer examples of the first three rewriting moves that I describe here: *coming to terms, forwarding* and *countering*. (You may find a single text that offers examples of two or more of these moves.) Mark those moments in the text where you see the writer making these moves, and be ready to talk about what you see him or her as doing.

You may also want to see if you can find instances of writers making moves with other texts that my terms *don't* seem to describe very well. What other terms might you offer in their place?

I then turn in chapter 4 to a form of rewriting that is at once generous and critical, in which you adopt, extend, and rework the driving questions and concerns of another writer. In *taking an approach,* you do not merely make use of a particular insight or concept from another writer (as in forwarding) but draw on his or her distinctive style or mode of working. This form of rewriting often involves applying a theory or method of analysis advanced by another writer to a new set of issues or texts. But you can also build on the insights of another writer, ask the sort of questions she might ask, draw on her characteristic uses of words and ideas, adapt her *style* of thought and writing to the demands of your own project—in ways that are at once more subtle and powerful. In this chapter I offer some strategies for working assertively in the mode of another writer, of taking an approach and making it your own.

Coming to terms, forwarding, countering, and *taking an approach* describe four ways of rewriting the work of others. In chapter 5 I suggest that you can also make use of these four moves in returning to and rewriting your *own* work-in-progress—a move that teachers of writing have for some time called *revising.* But while there has been much talk about the importance of revision, there has been little substantive advice on how to do it. Scholars like Peter Elbow and Donald Murray have offered excellent advice on drafting, on moving from nothing to something, getting words onto a page or screen. Others like Joseph Williams and Richard Lanham have written wonderful books on editing for style and clarity. But their focus has centered on reworking the form of sentences and paragraphs. Much less has been said about how to develop and revise a line of thinking over a series of *drafts.* That is what I try to offer in the last chapter of this book—an

Intertexts

Peter Elbow, *Writing with Power,* 2nd ed. (New York: Oxford University Press, 1998).

Donald Murray, *A Writer Teaches Writing,* 2nd ed. (Boston: Heinle, 2003).

Joseph Williams, *Style: Ten Lessons in Clarity and Grace,* 7th ed. (New York: Longman, 2002).

Richard Lanham, *Revising Prose,* 4th ed. (Boston: Allyn & Bacon, 1999).

approach to revising that asks you to question and rework your own writing much as you might do with the texts of others. How might you summarize your own draft, come to terms with what you have to say in it? How do you define your own project in relation to those of the texts you are discussing? At what moments in your text do you most clearly articulate your own line of thinking? How might you extend or forward this line? How might you qualify or even counter it? In posing such questions, I hope to sketch a view of revising as a systematic practice, a consistent set of moves that you can apply to your own writing-in-progress.

As you will have noted by now, I have also interspersed two sorts of notes throughout my text. The boxes marked *Intertexts* refer you to the reading that underlies this book—both by providing bibliographic information about the texts I use as examples and by acknowledging those writers and colleagues who have helped me formulate my ideas about writing. The boxes marked *Projects* gesture toward some of the uses I imagine that you might make of this book, toward some possible ways of taking my approach and forwarding or countering it for your own purposes. What appears in these two sets of boxes would usually be found in the notes, appendices, or bibliographies of other books—that is, buried at the bottom of their pages or stuffed near their back covers. But since my aim here is to illustrate how academic writers reuse and respond to other texts, I thought it would be useful to make the interplay of texts that animates *this* book a visible part of its pages.

What you won't find in the *Projects* boxes are conventional essay assignments. That's because I hope that this book will be used in a course in which you are already involved in reading and writing responses to other texts—to academic books and articles, fiction, movies, essays, plays, and the like. My aim is not to replace that sort of work with this book but to help you do it. Indeed, it seems to me that much as a piece of writing always needs to be about something, so, too, a writing *course* needs a subject, to be centered on some substantive issue or question—on the role of media in society, for instance, or the nature of work, or theories of schooling, or any of a thousand other complex and open issues that a group of writers can explore together. A book like this cannot provide such a subject or focus. Similarly, if a writing class is going to function as a class, this means that its members need to share and discuss the work that they are all doing as writers. Some readers have thus asked me why this book does not, until the last chapter on revising, include examples of student texts. My answer is that I hope that students using this book will look for such examples in the texts they are themselves writing. The kind of writing course that I teach brings three sets of texts to the table: (1) a group of readings that frame the subject—media, work, schooling, and so on—that we will look at together that semester; (2) the essays that students in the class draft and revise in response to those readings; and (3) other texts that discuss writing itself. This book is intended to fit into that third category.

I have more to say about such matters in the afterword on *teaching rewriting.* There I briefly describe some courses I have taught, both in composition and literature, that aim to help students imagine themselves as critics and intellectuals—that is, in which they are asked to read a wide range of texts, to connect what they read to their own interests and concerns, and to situate what they have to say in relation to the views of others. I describe the kinds of readings I like to work with and the types of writing projects I tend to assign. This afterword is addressed directly to teachers of academic writing—and so if I were a student in course using this book, it would be the first section I turned to. But it is really no more a teacher's guide than the rest of *Rewriting* is a textbook; there are no answers in the back, simply more ideas about writing and teaching.

Let me be as clear as I can about some other things that this book is *not.* It is not a guide to research; there are many such books already, and some very good ones, too. My concerns here begin at more or less the point when research ends: when you are faced with the question of what to say about a text that you have located or that you have been assigned to read. Neither do I have much to tell you about documenting sources or avoiding plagiarism; there are also plenty of handbooks that do that very well. And this is not a

Intertexts

Wayne C. Booth, Gregory C. Colomb, and Joseph M. Williams offer an excellent guide to *The Craft of Research*, 2nd ed. (Chicago: University of Chicago Press, 2003).

guide to the conventions that structure writing in the academic disciplines; indeed, the kind of writing that I talk about here is "academic" only in the sense that it tends to be taught in college. (If you are reading this, you are probably doing so for a course.) The sort of writing that I am drawn to strives to be part of public life. It's prose addressed not to academic specialists but to general readers—the sort of writing you find in *Harper's* and the *Atlantic* and the *Nation*, or in *Rolling Stone* and *McSweeney's* and *Salon*, as well as in independent weeklies, little magazines, student journals, some political and cultural blogs and websites, and the like. It's what I will often call here *intellectual prose*—with the caveat that by *intellectual* I don't mean wonkish or bohemian. I am interested in a kind of writing about texts and ideas, culture and politics, that while often associated with the academy, is not confined to it, that seeks instead to address a broader and more public set of issues and readers.

Projects

Coming to Terms with Rewriting

One way of coming to terms with a text is to make a list of its key terms and concepts and then to try to define them in your own words. (I will have more to say about such strategies in the first chapter.) As a way of articulating your own sense of what this book seems to be about, then, jot down at least four or five terms—*excluding* the titles of chapters—that strike you as important to my project here as a writer. Then see if you can write a paragraph in which you use those terms in describing the aims of this book (as best as you can now tell). You may want to return to this paragraph after you've finished reading this book—not so much to check your understanding of my work as to see if I have managed to achieve what I set out to do as writer.

Finally, I need say something about two other terms that are central to this book—one a specialized term and the other a word so familiar that some of its meanings have been dulled by use. The specialized term is *text*, by which I simply mean an artifact that holds meaning for some readers, viewers, or listeners. A book (or other piece of writing) is a text, but so are movies, plays, songs, paintings, sculptures, photographs, cartoons, videos, billboards, advertisements, web pages, and the like—as well as objects like buildings, cars, clothes, furniture, toys, games, and other gadgets when they have somehow acquired meaning for their users. But not everything is a text. Unlike actions, memories, or events, texts are objects that have been made and designed—*artifacts* that can in some way be shelved, filed, or stored and then retrieved and reexamined. That is what makes them so central to academic work. We may not agree on what a certain text means, but we can return to it and try to point to those specific aspects—lines, images, phrases, scenes—that lead us to interpret it differently. Someone else should always be able to check on how you have quoted a text.

The more commonplace but equally troublesome term is *interest*. I have often heard teachers remark that describing a piece of writing as "interesting" is to say very little about it, but I don't think that this needs to be the case. The critic Raymond Williams has shown how over time the word *interest* has acquired several layers of meaning: Its first recorded uses, in the sixteenth century, appear in the realms of law and finance, as in the sense of "holding an interest" in a company or "earning interest" from an investment. But early on the word also gained a more political or partisan sense, as in the "interests of state," "self-interest," or "an interested party." (The opposite of this meaning is "disinterested," like a judge.) But *interest* did not gain its most current meaning, of attracting curiosity or attention, until the nineteenth century. (The opposite here is "uninteresting" or dull.) I find all three of these meanings useful in thinking about a piece of writing. That is, you can ask of an essay: (1) How does this writer add interest or value to what has been

Intertexts

See Raymond Williams, *Keywords: A Vocabulary of Culture and Society,* rev. ed. (New York: Oxford University Press, 1983), 171–73, as well as the usage notes for *interest* in the online *Oxford English Dictionary.*

said before? (2) What is her interest in this issue, what perspective is she speaking for? and (3) How is her style in writing of interest or note? And so when I say that my aim in this book is to help you make *interesting* use of the work of others, I use the term in all three senses. I hope, that is, to help you write with perspicacity and wit about texts and issues that matter to you.

Projects

The Job of an Introduction

The test of an effective intro, then, is straightforward: Does it offer readers a strong sense of your aim and plan as a writer? Note that this question implies nothing about the correct form of an introduction—about what should go into first paragraphs or where claims or theses should be placed—and that is because the key issue here isn't structure but *function*. The point of an intro is to tell readers what is at stake and what to expect in your writing. The question is thus not what the proper form of an intro is but if it gets that job done.

I encourage you to test this view against your own reading. Look closely at the beginning pages of a number of academic books or articles (including, perhaps, this one): Are there any opening moves that all of the writers make? If so, do they make these moves at similar moments or in similar ways? And what changes from piece to piece? What sorts of things do the writers do differently as each works to define a project and plan?

I

Coming to Terms

A few weeks ago my old friend Dick Lower sent me this huge pile of
paper, saying that, as I am a voracious collector of curios and such-
like, perhaps I should have it. . . . How is a mere chronicler such as
myself to transmute the lead of inaccuracy in these papers into the
gold of truth?

— Iain Pears, *An Instance of the Fingerpost*

"The question is," said Alice, "whether you can make words mean
so many different things."

"The question is," said Humpty Dumpty, "which is to be mas-
ter—that's all."

— Lewis Carroll, *Through the Looking Glass*

I n his short story "Pierre Menard, Author of the *Quixote*," Jorge Luis
Borges tells of an obscure modern artist who decides to rewrite a passage from *Don Quixote,* the famous seventeenth-century novel by
Miguel de Cervantes. What makes this goal interesting, and more than a
little crazy, is that Menard doesn't want simply to copy or transcribe the
Quixote but instead "to produce a number of pages which coincided—word
for word and line for line—with those of Miguel de Cervantes." And to
make matters even more difficult, he resolves to do so without referring
back to the text of the *Quixote* or conducting any research on Cervantes.

To be a popular novelist of the seventeenth century in the twentieth
seemed to Menard to be a diminution. Being, somehow, Cervantes,

Intertexts

Jorge Luis Borges, "Pierre Menard, Author of the *Quixote*," in *Collected Fictions*, trans. Andrew Hurley (New York: Penguin, 1998), 88–95.

and arriving thereby at the Quixote—that looked to Menard less challenging (and therefore less interesting) than continuing to be Pierre Menard and coming to the Quixote *through the experiences of Pierre Menard.*

It's an absurd project, to write as your own part of a book that has already been written by someone else, and one that the narrator of Borges's story (who seems no less eccentric than Menard) admits was never completed. And yet, when the narrator rereads *Don Quixote* as though it were written not by Cervantes but by his friend, he finds that while the two versions are (of course) "verbally identical," the one composed by Menard seems "almost infinitely richer"—since one is no longer reading a romantic novel from another time and place but a contemporary text written *as if* it were such a work. Why would someone write or read such an odd text? Well, as the narrator observes, "ambiguity is richness."

Projects

Rereading Borges

Read "Pierre Menard" with the aim of assessing my use of it here. What aspects of this short fiction do I emphasize? What do I gloss over or omit? How might you add to or counter my reading of Borges?

There are few things harder to do than to explain a joke without seeming a bore, and I am aware that I have started this chapter by trying to do just that. "Pierre Menard, Author of the *Quixote*" offers pleasures to its readers that no summary can replicate, as Borges subtly and affectionately mocks the wild ambitions of writers, the pretensions of critics, and the backstage politics of the literary world. And certainly it's hard to take either Menard or his friend and biographer as seriously as they take themselves. But even still, I think that for all its ironies, Borges's story also hints at a theory of reading—

which is that to understand a text you need, in a way, to rewrite it, to take the ideas and phrasings of its author and turn them into your own. Texts don't simply reveal their meanings to us; we need to *make* sense of them. Like Menard, each of us comes at what we read through our own experiences and concerns, and so each of us makes a slightly different sense of the texts we encounter. We all write our own *Quixote*—at least to some degree. There is no such thing as a completely accurate and objective summary, a view from nowhere. All readings are interested (including my own here of Borges).

But if you cannot be neutral as a reader, you can strive to be fair and self-reflective. This is why I find it helpful to think of the kind of rewriting in which you strive to represent the work of another, to translate the language and ideas of a text into words of your own, as a *coming to terms*— since, among other things, the phrase suggests a settling of accounts, a negotiation between reader and writer. In coming to terms, you need both to give a text its due and to show what uses you want to make of it. You are not simply re-presenting a text but incorporating it into your own project as a writer. You thus need not only to explain what you think it means but to say something about the perspective from which you are reading it. In coming to terms with the work of others, then, you also say a good deal about who you are as a writer, about your own interests and values.

Of course, the idea of coming to terms also emphasizes that we are dealing here with words, with connecting your language to that of the texts you are reading. Such work involves a dialectic between paraphrase and quotation. On the one hand, to make strong use of the work of another writer, you need to be able to restate what she or he has to say in your own terms, to offer your own paraphrase of her or his project. On the other hand, you also need to attend closely to the specific features of the texts you deal with, to note and respect their key moves and phrasings—or you run the risk of turning every text you read into a version of what you already want to say.

In coming to terms with a text by another writer, then, it seems to me that you need to make three moves:

- Define the *project* of the writer in your own terms.
- Note *keywords* or passages in the text.
- Assess the *uses and limits* of this approach.

I will discuss these three moves in detail in the rest of this chapter. Before I do so, though, I need to say that simply because this is the first chapter doesn't mean that coming to terms with other texts is always the first thing you need to do as an academic writer. There are few things more tedious to read than an essay in which a writer spends so much time carefully summarizing and restating the work of others that, in the end, you're left unsure about what he or she actually wanted to bring to the conversation. Good writers thus often draw quickly on terms and ideas from other thinkers. In writing an academic essay, though, there is usually a set of texts and perspectives that you need to consider at some length so that you can define your own views in relation to them. Such work is not always done at the start of an essay or in some other, closely demarcated section of it, like a "literature review"; instead, you are likely to find that you need to slow down and think through the views and phrasings of others at various points in a piece you are writing. And although I will keep my examples here brief, you can't always expect to come to terms with a text or a writer in the space of a paragraph or two. Some views and texts you encounter will almost surely seem to call for a much more sustained analysis and response. But even if executing them may sometimes become more complex, I think that the three central moves that you need to make in coming to terms with a text—defining projects, noting keywords, assessing uses and limits—stay the same.

Defining the Project of a Writer

"Who's against shorthand? No one I know. Who wants to be shortchanged? No one I know." So said the New Jersey poet and doctor William Carlos Williams to another doctor and writer, the psychiatrist Robert Coles. Williams's remark appears in an essay by Coles, "Stories and Theories," in which he warns against the damage that can be done when complex views and experiences are reduced to easy labels. And yet, to respond to another text you *have* to summarize it, put its key phrasings and ideas in some kind of shorthand. So how do you do that without shortchanging it, too?

The usual advice is to restate the "main idea" or "thesis" of a text.

> **Intertexts**
>
> Robert Coles, "Stories and Theories," in *The Call of Stories* (Boston: Houghton Mifflin, 1989).

Such advice imagines a piece of writing as something fixed or static, as an argument that a writer has "constructed" or a position that she has "defended"—and which can thus be condensed and reified into something like a "thesis statement." But there are many writers who don't so much argue for a single claim or position as *think through* a complex set of texts and problems. Their books and essays offer not sharply defined positions but ways of talking about a subject. The questions to ask of such work draw on metaphors of movement and growth: What issues drive this essay? What ideas does it explore? What lines of inquiry does it develop? To try to reduce this kind of open-ended text to a single main idea or claim would almost certainly be to shortchange it.

Instead the question to ask is: What is the writer trying *to do* in this text? What is his or her *project?* A *project* is usually something far more complex than a main idea, since it refers not to a single concept but to a plan of work, to a set of ideas and questions that a writer "throws forward" (Latin, *pro + jacare*). The idea of a project thus raises questions of intent. A project is something that a writer is working on—and that a text can only imperfectly realize. (Of course, any text you write will also hint at possibilities of meaning you had not considered, imply or suggest things you had not planned. A text always says both less and more than its writer intends.) To define the project of a writer is thus to push beyond his text, to hazard a view about not only what someone has said but also what he was trying to accomplish by saying it.

An example may help here. In her book *In a Different Voice*, Carol Gilligan shows how mainstream theories of psychology stumble in helping us understand why women respond to moral conflicts in ways that often differ from men. Gilligan doesn't suggest that previous generations of psychologists were wrong but rather that their views of the self were shaped and limited by their focus on the development of men. And so here, for instance, is how she approaches a seminal essay by Sigmund Freud:

> In 1914, with his essay "On Narcissism," Freud swallows his distaste at the thought of "abandoning observation for barren theoretical controversy" and extends his map of the psychological domain. Tracing the development of the capacity to love, which he equates with maturity and psychic health, he locates its origins in the contrast between love for the mother and love for the self. But in thus dividing the world between

Intertexts

Carol Gilligan, *In a Different Voice: Psychological Theory and Women's Development* (Cambridge: Harvard University Press, 1982), 24.

Freud's "On Narcissism" (1914) is reprinted in *The Standard Edition of the Complete Psychological Works,* vol. 14, ed. and trans. James Strachey (London: Hogarth, 1961).

narcissism and "object" relationships, he finds that while men's development becomes clearer, women's becomes increasingly opaque. The problem arises because the contrast between mother and self yields two different images of relationships. Relying on the imagery of men's lives in charting the course of human growth, Freud is unable to trace in women the development of relationships, morality, or a clear sense of self. This difficulty of fitting the logic of his theory to women's experience leads him in the end to set women apart, marking their relationships, like their sexual life, as "a 'dark continent' for psychology."

The first thing I'd note about this passage is its generosity. Gilligan is describing a view that she feels is deeply flawed, that indeed she is writing her book in an effort to correct, but her goal here seems to be to offer an account of Freud's thinking that he might have himself agreed with. Even the problem with his theory that she points out is one that Freud himself recognized, as Gilligan makes clear by quoting his comment about women remaining a "dark continent" for psychology. This isn't to say that her view of Freud is disinterested. Gilligan is trying to clear space in this passage for her own study of women's moral growth through showing how his theories are grounded in the experiences of men alone. In giving Freud his due, she lends a sense of weight to her own response to his work.

Gilligan does not so much summarize "On Narcissism" as describe Freud's aims and strategies in writing it. The subject or actor of nearly every one of her sentences is Freud—whom Gilligan pictures as "swallowing his distaste" about theory, "extending his map" of psychology, "tracing the development" of love, "locating its origins," and so on. In doing so, she describes "On Narcissism" less as a structure supporting a single main idea than as a series of moves that Freud makes as a writer. One strength of this approach is stylistic: We tend to find it easier to follow prose that offers a narrative than prose that elaborates a set of abstract propositions—and

Gilligan here offers us a brief story of ideas with Freud at its center. More important, to describe his plan of work, Gilligan needs to say something about Freud's *aims, methods,* and *materials*. This allows her, in her brief account of his essay, both to honor his project and to begin to point to some of its problems—through representing what he was trying to do (trace the origins of love), how he did it (examining the child's relationship with his mother), and where his data or insights came from (the early experiences of male children).

You can ask much the same questions in defining the projects of other writers:

- *Aims:* What is a writer trying to achieve? What position does he or she want to argue? What issues or problems does he or she explore?
- *Methods:* How does a writer relate examples to ideas? How does he or she connect one claim to the next, build a sense of continuity and flow?
- *Materials:* Where does the writer go for examples and evidence? What texts are cited and discussed? What experiences or events are described?

And, to follow Gilligan's lead once again, you need to ask and answer these questions in a generous mode. To make effective use of the work of other writers, you have to show the force of their thinking, to suggest in your rewriting of their work *why* they said what they said in the particular ways they said it. And the best way to do that is to pay close attention to how their texts are worded.

Noting Keywords and Passages

One mark of a strong academic writer is the ability to move from the global to the local, from projects to phrasings, from talking about a text as a whole to noticing moments of particular interest in it. To come to terms with a complex text you need to be able to shift levels in this way, to ground how you define the project of a writer by citing key passages from his or her text. Such quotations may often be short and pointed. If you return to Gilligan's paragraph on Freud, for instance, you'll note that she quotes the language of his essay at only three points, and each time quite briefly: once to show that Freud was concerned that in "On Narcissism" he was entering the realm of "theoretical controversy," another time to note the key concept of "object" relations, and a final time to show that he was aware that his views had turned the experiences of women into a "dark continent." (In each case, the words quoted are Freud's.) While these touches are light, they are also crucial: Delete them, and one might ask, "But is that really what Freud said?" Keep them, and even if you disagree with her account of Freud, you still need to admit that Gilligan has noticed something about his text and project.

There is a subtle but important distinction to make here: You don't quote from a text to explain what it means in some neutral or objective way. *You quote from a text to show what your perspective on it makes visible.* If we all read a text in the same way, there'd be little need for us to argue over the meaning of its specific lines or phrasings. But academic writing is based on the idea that we read texts differently. Intellectuals often discuss books and articles that their readers are familiar with, and sometimes may even know quite well. But the interest of an academic essay usually has less to with its subject than with the approach of its writer. You don't need to reexplain a text to somebody who has already read it. But you can offer a different way of reading that text, to point out how your perspective allows you to notice something new about it.

In deciding when to quote, then, the question to ask is not *What is the writer of this text trying to say?* but *What aspects of this text stand out for me as a reader?* Quote to illustrate your view of a text, to single out terms or passages that strike you in some way as interesting, troubling, ambiguous, or suggestive. Weak academic essays are often marked by an overreliance on quotation, as the words of the authors quoted begin to drown out those of the person writing about them. You don't want the writers you quote to do your work for you. You want the focus of your readers instead to be on your ideas, to draw their attention not to the texts you're quoting but to the work you're doing *with* those texts. And so, when what you need to do is to restate what a certain writer is trying to do, to represent her or his project, try to paraphrase the work as quickly and accurately as you can. Save quotation for moments that advance your project, your view of the text.

Or let me put it this way: Summarize when what you have to say about a text is routine and quote when it is more contentious. Here, for instance, is I. F. Stone, in *The Trial of Socrates*, pointing to what he sees as a key difference between the worldviews of the ancient Greek philosophers Aristotle and Plato:

> Plato was a theorist, Aristotle a scientific observer. Aristotle prized practical over theoretical knowledge in dealing with human affairs. Aristotle had a strong bias in favor of experience and common sense. In contrast, Plato in a famous passage of *The Republic* proposed to limit his study of "the dialectic"—and thus the future rulers of his utopia—to those who could "let go of the eyes and other senses and rise to the contemplation of *to on*"—"pure being" or "being itself." This would no doubt be a contemplative joy to the mystic, but it hardly offers guidance to the statesman, forced to deal with tangled affairs and obdurate human nature.
>
> Aristotle takes issue with Plato at the very beginning of his own masterwork on philosophy, the *Metaphysics*. It starts off by saying, "All men naturally desire knowledge. An indication of this is our esteem for the senses." Without them, and especially sight, Aristotle asks, how can we know and act?

Plato and Aristotle both wrote many works, and their thought has been the focus of an uncountable number of commentaries over the past 2,500 years. (Alfred North Whitehead once remarked that European philosophy in large part "consists of a series of footnotes to Plato.") So there is no way that Stone (or anyone else) could possibly "prove" that Plato was a theorist and Aristotle an observer—at least not in terms quite so simple. But I don't understand that to be his aim in this passage. Rather, I think that what Stone wants to show is that there is a *way of looking* at Plato and Aristotle that is both reasonably fair to their work and useful to his own project. (He goes on later in his book to link Plato's bent for theory

Intertexts

I. F. Stone, *The Trial of Socrates* (Boston: Little, Brown, 1988), 13.

Stone quotes from the Loeb Classical Library editions of both Plato and Aristotle.

Whitehead's remark has itself been quoted (and often misquoted) in hundreds of other texts. It first appeared in his *Process and Reality*, rev. ed. (New York: Free Press, 1978), 39.

to the antidemocratic politics of his mentor, Socrates.) Stone makes the case for his approach through a pointed use of quotation, contrasting Plato's exhortation to "let go of the eyes and other senses" with Aristotle's "esteem for the senses." These sentences do not summarize the work of either philosopher. No sentence or two ever could. Rather, they illustrate Stone's particular view of the differences between Plato and Aristotle. They are salient moments from his perspective as a reader. They show him rewriting their work as part of his own project.

You'll have noticed that I say of Stone's approach that it seems "reasonably fair" to Plato and Aristotle. Those may seem waffle words, but I don't mean them as such. On the contrary, the question of what counts as a fair reading lies at the center of much academic argument. Several of Stone's critics felt that he failed to represent the work of Plato and Socrates very well, just as some of Gilligan's readers thought that she misunderstood Freud. Such disagreements are inevitable. The best you can do as a reader is to try to show *why* you view a text in a certain way, both in terms of the values you bring to the text and the moments you notice in it. Your readers can then point to different values and different moments, and your ways of reading the text can then be contrasted and argued for, if not resolved.

You can see quotations as *flashpoints* in a text, moments given a special intensity, made to stand for key concepts or issues. A useful rule of thumb, then, is to quote only those phrases or passages that you want to do further work with or bring pressure upon—whose particular implications and resonances you want to analyze, elaborate, counter, revise, echo, or transform. Such pressure does not have to be skeptical; you can quote from a text in order to highlight the power of a particular way of phrasing an issue. For instance, here is Cornel West, philosopher and cultural critic, near the start of his book *Race Matters*:

> The common denominator of these views of race is that each still sees black people as a "problem people," in the words of Dorothy I. Height, president of the National Council of Negro Women, rather than as fellow American citizens with problems. Her words echo the poignant "unasked question" of W. E. B. Du Bois, who, in *The Souls of Black Folk* (1903), wrote:

They approach me in a half-hesitant way, eye me curiously or compassionately, and then instead of saying directly, How does it feel to be a problem? they say, I know an excellent colored man in my town . . . Do not these Southern outrages make your blood boil? At these I smile, or am interested, or reduce the boiling to a simmer, as the occasion may require. To the real question, How does it feel to be a problem? I answer seldom a word.

Intertexts

Cornel West, *Race Matters* (Boston: Beacon, 1993), 2–3.
  The Souls of Black Folk (1903) is reprinted in *The Oxford W .E. B. DuBois Reader* (New York: Oxford University Press, 1996). The passage quoted is found on p. 101. West does not provide a reference for the Height quotation.

Nearly a century later, we confine discussions about race in America to the "problems" black people pose for whites rather than considering what this way of viewing black people reveals about us as a nation.

This paralyzing framework encourages liberals to relieve their guilty consciences by supporting public funds directed at "the problems"; but at the same time, reluctant to exercise principled criticism of black people, liberals deny them freedom to err. Similarly, conservatives blame the "problems" on black people themselves—and thereby render black social misery invisible or unworthy of public attention.

Making use of the words of Height, DuBois, and others, West constructs a jazzlike progression that moves from "problem people" to "citizens with problems" to "how does it feel to be a problem?" to "the 'problems' black people pose" to "the problems" to "blame the 'problems' on black people themselves." I especially admire the finesse with which he distinguishes between the "problems" that liberals see as besetting blacks and the "problems" that conservatives see blacks as causing. The net effect of these echoes-with-a-difference is to give the word *problem,* as it is used in discussions of race, a rich and disturbing complexity of meanings. West uses a series of quotations to pull the term out of general usage, as it were, and to grant it instead a particular history and meaning, to ask his readers to consider how race poses a specific and unusual sort of "problem" for us.

Quotation thus has two distinct uses in coming to terms with the work of another writer. On the one hand, it can serve as a *brake* on paraphrase. In quoting key passages from a text, you show respect for the specificity of its tone, ideas, and phrasings. You make it clear that you have not carelessly substituted its language with your own. On the other hand, quotation can *intensify* paraphrase. It allows you to scrutinize particular moments in a text—to suggest either the usefulness of a certain way of phrasing an issue (as West does with "problem") or its limitations (as Gilligan does with Freud's "dark continent"). I will return to this second use of quotation in the following chapters—since bringing pressure on a writer's phrasings is a crucial aspect of forwarding, countering, or transforming her project. For now, though, I need to say a little more about *coming to terms* as a form of reckoning or negotiation.

Assessing Uses and Limits

We live in a culture prone to naming winners and losers, rights and wrongs. You're in or out, hot or not, on the bus or off it. But academics seldom write in an all-or-nothing mode, trying to convince readers to take one side or the other of an argument. Instead their work assumes that any perspective on an issue (and there are often more than two) will have moments of both insight and blindness. A frame offers a view but also brackets something out. A point of view highlights certain aspects and obscures others. And so, in dealing with other writers, your aim should be less to prove them right or wrong, correct or mistaken, than to assess both the uses and limits of their work. That is to say, academic writing rarely involves a simple taking of sides, an attack on or defense of set positions, but rather centers on a weighing of options, a sorting through of possibilities.

In writing as an intellectual, then, you need to push beyond the sorts of bipolar oppositions (pro or con, good or evil, guilty or innocent) that frame most of the arguments found on editorial pages and TV talk shows. Intellectual writers usually work not with simple antitheses (either *x* or *not-x*) but with *positive opposing terms*—that is, with words and values that don't contradict each other yet still exist in some real and ongoing tension. For instance, I have suggested in this chapter that you need to deal with the work of others in ways that are both *generous* and *assertive*. These terms are not direct opposites, but neither are they congruent. Rather, they name different and competing values in writing that I believe you need to learn to negotiate. Or, for another example, you might look back at the piece on "Stories and Theories" by Robert Coles that I mentioned earlier. In that essay, Coles distinguishes between two kinds of discourse: *stories,* which we use in evoking the felt quality of events, and *theories,* which we use in analyzing their meanings. A story is not merely a bad version of a theory or vice versa. The two words describe distinct uses of language, each with its own strengths and weaknesses. They are positive opposing terms.

Academic writers often bring a cluster of texts and perspectives into this sort of positive opposition or tension. This is more complex and interesting work than simply taking sides in a debate, since it involves thinking through the potential uses of a number of positions rather than arguing for or against a fixed point of view. In coming to terms with a text, then, the key questions to ask have to do not with correctness but use. What does this text do or see well? What does it stumble over or occlude?

Here, for instance, is how John Seely Brown and Paul Duguid, in their book on *The Social Life of Information,* approach the work of one of their colleagues:

Let us begin by taking a cue from MIT's Nicholas Negroponte. His handbook for the information age, *Being Digital,* encouraged everyone to think about the differences between atoms, a fundamental unit of matter, and bits, and the fundamental unit of information. Here was a provocative and useful thought experiment in contrasts. Moreover, it can be useful to consider possible similarities between the two as well.

Consider, for example, the industrial revolution, the information revolution's role model. It was a period in which society learned how to process, sort, rearrange, recombine, and transport atoms in unprecedented fashion. Yet people didn't complain that they were drowning in atoms. They didn't worry about atom overload. Because, of course, while the world may be composed of atoms, people don't perceive it that way. They perceive it as buses and books and tables and chairs, buildings and coffee mugs, laptops and cell phones, and so forth. Similarly, while information may come to us in quadrillions of bits, we don't consider it that way. The information reflected in bits comes to us, for example, as stories, documents, diagrams, pictures, or narratives, as knowledge and meaning, and in communities, organizations, and institutions.

The strength of this passage hinges on that *moreover* near the end of the first paragraph. Brown and Duguid use this term to signal a complex stance toward Negroponte. They don't deny the suggestiveness of the contrast he draws between atoms and bits; in fact, they play with and elaborate upon it. But they also suggest that there is something that this contrast fails to make visible, or may even hide—something that has to do with the structures and contexts in which atoms and bits are always embedded. They thus neither simply endorse nor reject his perspective but point out its uses and limits.

> **Intertexts**
>
> John Seely Brown and Paul Duguid, *The Social Life of Information* (Boston: Harvard Business School Press, 2000), 15-16.
>
> Brown and Duguid are discussing Nicholas Negroponte's *Being Digital* (New York: Basic Books, 1995).

They "take a cue" from Negroponte, that is, not by simply restating his view of how atoms and bits are different but by thinking more about their relationship and deciding that they can also be seen as similar. They come to terms with his work by showing both what he sees powerfully and what he fails to notice.

Indeed, you might use *moreover* as a catchword for much of the work of coming to terms with another text—in which you need not only to indicate what a writer does well but also to suggest what she or he has left undone. In arguing that academic writing needs to hold a number of competing views in tension, though, I don't mean to advocate tepid or bland prose. Rather, I am urging you to approach writing with an active mix of skepticism and generosity—both to look for gaps or difficulties in perspectives you admire and also to try to understand the strengths of those you don't. Form the habit of questioning your first responses: So, here's a text that seems to offer a compelling way of looking at an issue—what does it also bracket out of sight? Or, here's a text that seems curiously wrongheaded or obtuse—what might account for its seeming strangeness? what is its writer trying to accomplish? (If you really can't answer such questions, you're probably not dealing with a text that you can put to good use, since simply proving someone else wrong rarely advances your own thinking.) To forward the phrasings or ideas of other writers, you need to know what they can't do as well as what they can. And to counter the work of another, you need to recognize not just its limits but its strengths. I'll have more to say about those forms of rewriting in the next two chapters. My point here, though, is that to come to terms with a text, you need not only to restate its project but also to take its measure.

Projects

The Moves of Reviewing

Of the various moves I discuss in this book, coming to terms with a text is perhaps the only one that can often serve as the entire aim or purpose of certain kinds of writing— namely, of reviews, prefaces, cover or liner notes, blurbs and notices, annotated bibliographies, and the like. The whole point of such forms of writing is to describe and assess other texts.

In a consumer culture, such review texts are ubiquitous. You can find them in newspapers and magazines, on CD covers, book jackets, store posters, websites, and the like.

Locate one and describe the moves its writer makes in presenting the text she or he is discussing. In what ways do these techniques align with or differ from the moves (for coming to terms with another text as *part* of a larger essay) that I have discussed here?

Quotation: Some Terms of Art

This is not a handbook but a text that tries to think through some ways of working as a writer with the words, images, and ideas of others. I will thus not review here the many and arcane rules for punctuating quotations and citing sources—which, to my point of view, have more to do with typing than writing and which, in any case, vary widely from one context to the other. The best advice I can offer you is to ask your teacher or editor what manual or style sheet you need to follow, buy a copy, and consult it carefully in preparing the final version of your work. There are plenty of details but few intellectual issues involved in compiling a list of references or works cited; it's the kind of thing you want to get right the first time. The same goes for citing sources and page numbers. Most academic disciplines now use some version of parenthetical or in-text citation rather than footnotes, in which you place key information about a text you've quoted (name, author, page number, etc.) in parentheses following the quotation. If a reader then wants to look up the text you've quoted, he or she can consult its fuller entry in your list of works cited. Exactly what information should go in these parentheses, in what order, with what sorts of punctuation, as well as where the parentheses themselves should be placed in your own sentence—the answers to such questions can once again vary widely from one context or discipline to the next. The only way to make sure you get it right is to learn what style sheet to use. After that, pretty much the only thing you need to do is to follow the format it lays out.

But how you actually go about incorporating other texts into your own prose can also say a good deal about the stance or attitude you want to take toward them, and in ways that cannot be reduced to a simple matter of rules. There is, for instance, the question of how much you want to emphasize the *otherness* of the texts you quote, to what degree you want to make the difference between their language and yours visible on the page. The advice given by most writing manuals, it seems to me, urges you to downplay this sense of otherness, to quote in ways that work toward the illusion of a seamless text, incorporating the words of others as much as you can within your own sentences. On the other end of this spectrum is a text like the Vulgate Bible, which sets the words of Jesus in red type, separating them from the prose of the evangelists in a way that can be seen, literally, from across the room. My own sense, as I hope is suggested by the look and feel of this book, is that you want to develop a flexible repertoire of forms of quotation, including:

Intertexts

Several academic disciplines publish their own guides to documenting sources. Among those most often used are:

Joseph Gibaldi, *The MLA Handbook for Writers of Research Papers,* 5th ed. (New York: Modern Language Association, 1999). (literature)

The APA Publication Manual, 4th ed. (Washington, DC: American Psychological Association, 1994). (social sciences)

Kate Turabian, *A Manual for Writers of Term Papers, Theses, and Dissertations,* 6th ed. (Chicago: University of Chicago Press, 1996). Often simply called *Turabian,* this manual offers a version of the format defined by the voluminous *Chicago Manual of Style,* 15th ed. (University of Chicago Press, 2003). (humanities)

Most good handbooks provide brief guides to the MLA, APA, and Chicago styles.

- *Block quotes:* Setting or "blocking" off the text of another writer from your own. Most of the key examples in this book take this form. Block quotes are often indented from the main text and set in a different font and spacing. They are seldom framed with quotation marks. Block quotes tend to make the work of others highly visible in your writing. They are often used when you need to quote several lines from a work, but also, and more important, as a form of emphasis, as a way of saying that this is a text that you, as a writer, plan to return to and work more with.
- *In-text quotes:* Incorporating the words of another writer as part of your own text, while marking and framing your use of their

work with quotation marks. In-text quotes are most often used to note and emphasize particular terms and phrasings, to add to and qualify paraphrase. They are usually brief, although you may sometimes want to quote a full sentence or two without giving it the weight of a block quote. The rules for punctuating in-text quotes are byzantine and contested, although the basic principle is simple enough: Punctuation creates distance. A quotation introduced by a colon or a comma, or one that stands on its own as a sentence, feels more separate from your words and thinking than one that is dropped into the flow of your own prose with little or no punctuation.

- *Scare quotes:* Putting quotation marks around a word to signal that it is not one that you feel is apt. Scare quotes are the visual marker of sarcasm. They often refer not to a specific moment in a text but to a more general usage of a term. Cornel West makes effective use of them in the passage I quoted previously, when he says, "This paralyzing framework encourages liberals to relieve their guilty consciences by supporting public funds directed at 'the problems' . . . Similarly, conservatives blame the 'problems' on black people themselves." However, a little irony can go a long way. Often the best test is reading aloud. If you find yourself dropping your voice sententiously each time you reach a quoted term, consider limiting your use of scare quotes. Italics offer an alternative way of putting emphasis on a word without giving it a negative spin.

- *Epigraphs:* Setting a quotation at the head of a book, chapter, essay, or section of an essay. The term epigraph comes from the Greek, *epi + graphos,* "to write upon"; it thus refers literally to an inscription—as on a statue, gravestone, or building. Some of this meaning has carried over to its use in writing, as an epigraph is the one form of quotation that a writer is not expected to comment on. Rather, it is usually the epigraph that comments on the text that follows—that sets a tone or suggests a perspective, sometimes quite obliquely. When done well, an epigraph can serve as a kind of poetic précis of a text, summing up its aim or scope—even if its full meaning does not always become clear until the piece has been read through and the epigraph considered a second time. Done less well, epigraphs can sometimes appear self-importantly literary, too erudite by half.

- *Allusions:* Leaving a brief quotation unmarked, in the expectation that readers will hear the echo of the other text in your own. The term derives from the Latin, *ad* + *ludere*, "to play with," and suggests something more on the lines of a hint and a wink than a direct statement. Academic writing often routinely proceeds from direct quotation to a more mundane kind of allusion—as, for instance, when the work of a writer is introduced by means of a block quote, which is then followed by an analysis of key terms and passages that are quoted in text, and finally when those terms are used without quotation marks but still carrying a particular set of inflections and meanings. In *Race Matters,* for example, Cornel West follows the paragraph I've quoted with one that starts, "To engage in a serious discussion of race in America, we must begin not with the problems of black people but with the flaws of American society." By this point in his text, West has dropped the quotation marks from around *problem,* but his use of the term still clearly echoes those of Height, DuBois, and the "liberals" and "conservatives" that he has just cited. His prose alludes to a set of meanings that he no longer needs to quote.

Block quotes, in-text quotes, scare quotes, epigraphs, allusions—these are *terms of art,* words that the practitioners of a craft use to describe their work. In learning such terms, you acquire not simply a vocabulary but a sense of what distinctions matter in the practice of a craft. In this case, the range of terms used to describe forms of quotation speaks to the key role that dealing with the work of others plays in academic writing. The value placed on representing other texts accurately is further shown by the set of practices that academics have developed to show when a writer has needed to alter a quotation, however slightly—as with the use of ellipses (. . .) to mark a break in a quoted passage, of [brackets] to mark additions or changes made to a text, and of the notation (emphasis added) to indicate when terms in a passage have been italicized or otherwise highlighted. A strong use of the work of others is always grounded in a scrupulous care in citing their texts.

Coming to terms in some ways offers the clearest example of what I mean by *rewriting*. You come to terms with a text by translating its words and ideas into your own language, making them part of your own prose—not only re-presenting the work of another writer but also, at times, actually retyping it as you quote key terms and passages from a text. But I suspect that you will also find that in trying seriously to come to terms with another text, and especially in assessing its uses and limits, your focus as a writer soon shifts away from simply restating what that text has to say and toward the uses you can make of its concepts and phrases, or toward the gaps and problems you encounter in trying to do so. I will turn to such *forwarding* and *countering* moves in the next chapters.

Projects

Coming to Terms with Your Own Work-in-Progress

In chapter 5 I offer some ideas about how to apply each of the moves I discuss in this book to your own work as a writer. But you might also find it useful to begin to think now about how come to terms with a piece while you are in the process of drafting it.

The next time you complete the first full draft of a writing project, see if you can write a paragraph or two in which you describe your essay as it then stands. Don't think of yourself as writing a new introduction to your essay. Rather, imagine your task as coming to terms with your own work, representing your essay to someone who hasn't read it. In this brief piece, try to

- Define your aim in writing your draft.
- Comment on the present strengths and limits of your piece—those aspects or sections you're pleased with and those you want to work more on.

Such reflective pieces can often be surprisingly hard to write. But that is why they are useful, since the difficulties you meet in trying to come to terms with a draft may point you toward work you need to do in revising it. You may find, for instance, in the early stages of a piece, that you're not really sure yet what your aim in writing is—or that your aim is the fairly weak or uninteresting one of simply restating what some other writer has said. If so, you will then also know that you need to define your own project in writing more clearly. Or you might sense in the difficulties you have in mapping out an essay that there is something about your line of thinking that is not yet quite clear even to you—and thus that you need somehow to restructure your essay. Or you may realize that the texts you're working with, or the passages you're quoting from them, don't really help you make the points that you want—and thus that you need to rethink the evidence for the position you want to take. In coming to terms with an early draft of a project, that is, you can begin to form a plan for revising it.

ב

forwarding

The painter's products stand before us as though they were still alive, but if you question them, they maintain a most majestic silence. It is the same with written words; they seem to talk to you as if they were intelligent, but if you ask them anything about what they say, from a desire to be instructed, they go on telling you just the same thing forever.

—Plato, *Phaedrus*

The dead, thing-like text has potentials far outdistancing those of the simply spoken word.

—Walter Ong, "Writing Is a Technology That Restructures Thought"

Academic writing is often described as a kind of conversation. You read a text, you talk about it, you put down some thoughts in response, others respond to your comments, and so on. Or as the poet, novelist, philosopher, and critic Kenneth Burke once put it:

Imagine that you enter a parlor. You come late. When you arrive, others have long preceded you, and they are engaged in a heated discussion, a discussion too heated for them to pause and tell you exactly what it is about. In fact, the discussion has begun long before any of them got there, so that no one present is qualified to retrace for you all the steps that had gone on before. You listen for a while, until you decide that you have caught the tenor of the argument; then you put in your oar. Someone answers; you answer him; another comes to your defense;

34

another aligns himself against you, to either the embarrassment or gratification of your opponent, depending on the quality of your ally's assistance. The hour grows late, you must depart. And you do depart, with the discussion still vigorously in progress.

Intertexts

Kenneth Burke, *The Philosophy of Literary Form: Studies in Symbolic Action* (Berkeley: University of California Press, 1973), 110–11.

David Bartholomae, "Inventing the University," in *When A Writer Can't Write*, ed. Mike Rose (New York: Guilford, 1985), 134.

Others have drawn on this metaphor to imagine the various disciplines and professions as being, in effect, different sorts of conversations—each with its own rules of evidence and etiquette. In this view, to become a lawyer, a historian, a biologist, or a social worker, you need to learn to think and talk like a lawyer, a historian, a biologist, or a social worker. Learning a subject means acquiring a discourse, not just mastering a body of knowledge. As another teacher of academic writing, David Bartholomae, has argued:

> Every time a student sits down to write for us, he has to invent the university for the occasion—invent the university, that is, or a branch of it, like history or anthropology or economics or English. The student has to learn to speak our language, to speak as we do, to try on the peculiar ways of knowing, selecting, evaluating, reporting, concluding, and arguing that define the discourse of our community.

This metaphor of writing as conversation has several strengths. It highlights the social aspects of intellectual work, the ways in which academic writing responds to the texts and ideas of others. It suggests that the goal of such writing is not to have the final word on a subject, to bring the discussion to a close, but to push it forward, to say something new, something that seems to

Intertexts

In this sense, the passage I've quoted fails to suggest the larger aim of Burke's writing, which was to theorize a "rhetoric of courtship," a discourse that strives for agreement rather than confrontation, identification rather than division. See Kenneth Burke, *A Rhetoric of Motives* (Berkeley: University of California Press, 1969).

call for further talk and writing. And despite Burke's somewhat militaristic talk of allies and opponents, the metaphor also hints at the more civil tone of much academic work. A dialogue is not a debate. You don't win a conversation, you add to it, push it ahead, keep it going, "put your oar in," and maybe even sometimes redirect or divert the flow of talk. But you rarely win over a person you are speaking with by first refuting what she or he has just said. The arts of conversation are subtler than those of debate; they join our need to articulate the differences among us with our need to keep talking with one another.

But if academic writing is a conversation, then it is one of a curious and asymmetrical sort. For academics rarely write *to* the persons whose work they are writing *about*. If you are assigned in a class, for instance, to respond to a play by Shakespeare, you don't expect its author to write you back. Your writing is instead directed at other readers of the play. In quoting Shakespeare, then, you are less entering into conversation with him (whoever he may have been) than with fellow readers of his work (wherever they may now be). You are *recirculating* his writing, highlighting parts of his text for the consideration of others. And I'd argue that this is the case for most academic writing—that it does not reply to the texts it cites so much as *forward* passages and ideas from them.

Another way to put this might be to say that academic writing is almost always intended to persuade a *third* reader. One scholar will criticize the work of another less in the hope of having her rival recant than in persuading other readers to see the good sense of her (rather than his) views. Even an indignant author writing to protest a wrongheaded review of his latest book addresses his letter "To the Editor." If you *reply* to an email post you have received, you are engaging in a private correspondence. If you *forward*

> ## Intertexts
>
> "When it has once been written down, every discourse rolls about everywhere, reaching indiscriminately those with understanding no less than those who have no business with it, and it doesn't know to whom it should speak and to whom it should not. And when it is faulted and attacked unfairly, it always needs its father's support; alone, it can neither defend itself nor come to its own support."
> Plato, *Phaedrus*, trans. Alexander Nehamas and Paul Woodruff (Indianapolis: Hackett, 1995), 81 (275E).

that post (or part of it) to another set of readers, along with your comments on it, you have begun a more public exchange. In the email program I use, these two functions are illustrated by opposing arrows: reply (←) sends your comments back to the sender; forward (→) directs them outward to other readers. And these forwards can themselves be forwarded, to sometimes unexpected sites and publics—as anyone who has ever written an email post that seemed to take on a life of its own, found its way to unintended readers, can testify. The power of the Internet to make texts accessible comes with a cost, as you not only gain readers for a text but also lose control of its uses once you send it forward into the public sphere. (This was precisely the worry about writing voiced centuries ago by the philosopher Plato—that texts can become "fatherless," detached from their authors and interpreted recklessly.) Much of academic discourse thus tends to proceed sideways, as writers take ideas and phrases from what they have read and reuse them in approaching a different set of issues and texts.

As I write this book, for instance, I am sitting in a small room, before a laptop computer, surrounded by books, papers, and magazines—all of which I am, in some metaphorical sense, "in conversation with" (in much the same way I am also in conversation with you, my imagined reader). But what I am actually *doing* is working with a set of materials—looking for books on my shelves and flipping through them, folding pages over or marking them with Post-its, retyping passages, filing and retrieving printouts and photocopies, making notes in margins and on index cards, and, of course, composing, cutting, pasting, formatting, revising, and printing blocks of prose. I am, that is, for the most part, moving bits of text and paper around. I don't want to lose the metaphor of conversation entirely—writing is in a very real way a process of trying to say something to somebody. But a text is also an artifact; it is not only something you say but something you *make*. And so, even when your goal in writing is to enter into a kind of conversation about a subject, to form your own response to what others have had to say about it, the question remains of how to construct or assemble that response.

As I use the term, a writer *forwards* a text by taking words, images, or ideas from it and putting them to use in new contexts. In forwarding a text, you test the strength of its insights and the range and flexibility of its phrasings. You rewrite it through reusing some of its key concepts and phrasings. In this chapter, I will focus on rewriting in the spirit of the texts you are reading, of applying and extending their ideas and phrasings. And then, in the next chapter, I will look at more skeptical forms of rewriting, of bringing texts forward for criticism and counterstatement. But let me emphasize that this order is not in any way fixed—there is no need, that is, to always try to find something nice to say about a text before criticizing it. You might instead think of these two chapters as building on the moves I outlined in the previous chapter on coming to terms. In forwarding a text, you extend its *uses;* in countering a text, you note its *limits.* These two moves often double upon one another: In applying a text to new situations, that is, you are likely to also end up revising some of its key words and concepts, much as in countering the stance or phrasings of a text, you may well begin to see how some of its aims might be better realized.

Projects

Conversing in Writing

Find a listserv or blog whose topics interest you. Spend a few days following the exchanges on it. Note down those moments at which the members of the list or board really seem to be "conversing in writing" with each other, and also note points where they seem to be doing something else (forwarding, flaming, digressing, whatever). How useful is the metaphor of conversation in describing the exchanges you've observed? What does the metaphor distort or fail to describe?

In forwarding a text, you begin to shift the focus of your readers away from what its author has to say and toward your own project. Writers often describe themselves as drawing on or mining other texts for ideas and examples, but extracting such materials is only part of the job. You then need to shape them to your own purposes in writing. There are at least four ways of doing so:

- *Illustrating:* When you look to other texts for examples of a point you want to make.
- *Authorizing:* When you invoke the expertise or status of another writer to support your thinking.
- *Borrowing:* When you draw on terms or ideas from other writers to use in thinking through your subject.
- *Extending:* When you put your own spin on the terms or concepts that you take from other texts.

Illustrating provides you with material to think *about:* anecdotes, images, scenarios, data. Authorizing, borrowing, and extending are ways of finding things in other texts to think *with:* keywords, concepts, approaches, theories. I will discuss each of these four moves in more detail below. Remember, though, that when you forward an idea or passage from another text you need not simply to cite but to use it. If you look to another text for an example, you need to make it an example of what you have to say. If you take a term from another writer, you need to show what you take it to mean and how it contributes to what you are arguing.

Illustrating

Writing for school often starts with an assigned text: A teacher hands you a book or essay to read and tells you to write an essay about it. But this isn't always—or perhaps even usually—how intellectual work begins. The impetus for many projects lies instead not in a specific text but in a question or idea or issue that a writer wants to explore. (There are exceptions, of course: book reviews, studies of particular authors, etc.) Such work often begins with something closer to a hunch than a thesis. You might, for instance, notice how cell phones or email can sometimes seem to distance people from one another as much as connect them, or how some advertisements seem to promote not so much a product as an experience or sensibility. But to write about such questions, you need to find some texts that can help you focus your hunch, formulate the issue more precisely. You need some texts, that is, to use in thinking about your subject.

A few years ago, I was involved in editing a book of essays on the uses of popular culture in everyday life. In doing so, I was struck by how many

Intertexts

Todd Gitlin, "We Build Excitement," in *Watching Television,* ed. Todd Gitlin (New York: Pantheon, 1986); reprinted in Joseph Harris, Jay Rosen, and Gary Calpas, eds., *Media Journal: Reading and Writing about Popular Culture,* 2nd ed. (Boston: Allyn & Bacon, 1999), 378–80.

critics began their essays by recounting a particular scene or image from a movie, TV show, or advertisement. Here, for instance, is how Todd Gitlin starts his piece, "We Build Excitement":

> An electronic throb comes across the screen. Through a blue-black, haze-shrouded night city wanders the solitary figure of a young blond man. He is handsome in a blank way, expressionless, almost robotic. The city is deserted. In this science-fictional future, the man has left the present, society, the clutter of other people behind. Is he liberated? Troubled? The electronic pulse continues. Vapors hover in the street, catching the light. The man stalks through evacuated streets, seeking signs of life. Suddenly, he spins around as if startled by a sound. Overhead looms a billboard depicting—what posthistoric icon of the age? The new Dodge. The sight fills him with awe. The car slides off the billboard and out into the world. It has a life of its own; indeed, more life than his own. It pursues him, calls him, teases him; the car is the active agent. The two of them are alone in this vacated kingdom; he might be the last man in the world. Now he turns and goes after the Dodge, which gives him the slip. He follows it down a narrow street, but it's gone. And then, with the abruptness of a jump cut, he finds himself in the driver's seat. His blankness fades; it is a satisfied go-getter who now turns to us and grins. Instantly dystopia segues into utopia. Accepting the challenge of hypernew technology, the driver has earned his place in the proverbial fast lane. The car then accelerates at *Star Wars*—like warp velocity and takes off into ethereal hyperspace. "Dodge," says the closing logo after a breathless thirty seconds, "An American Revolution."

This is a remarkable passage. Beginning with the visual image of the "electronic throb . . . across the screen," Gitlin intrudes on our consciousness much as the Dodge commercial does: suddenly and assertively. His short sentences evoke a sense of speed and fragmentation in tandem with a set of neologisms (*haze-shrouded, posthistoric, hypernew*) that hint at the futuristic feel of the thirty-second spot he is describing. His prose thus responds to one of the particular challenges of writing about nonprint me-dia—which is the need to re-present the texts you discuss, to translate them into language that begins to evoke the experience of viewing or listening to them. You can't reproduce a television ad or a movie scene on the page in the way you can recopy the words of a print text. Quoting the lyrics of a song doesn't always get at how it feels to hear it performed, and describing the subject of a photograph or painting can only begin to suggest its total impact as an image. Even the ability to scan or embed audio and visual files into electronic documents fails to solve this problem completely—although it does make writing about such texts more rigorous and interesting—since in order to comment on an aspect of an image or performance you still need somehow to put it in words.

In some ways, the difficulty of quoting nonprint media highlights the central problem of dealing with the texts of others: You need somehow to make their work yours. Faced with the impossibility of rendering the whole of an image or performance in words, you can only instead point to what you see as its key moments or features. That is to say, in describing a movie or song or ad, you need to interpret as you describe, to re-present the text in a way that shows how it illustrates the point you want to argue. A few more paragraphs into his essay, for instance, Gitlin's motives in describing the advertisement for Dodge start to become clear:

> Altogether this style of urgent and displaced velocity represented the most striking innovation in the automotive sales pitch of the mid-eighties. All the fancy-free varieties of the high-tech format bore the implication the car today is the carrier of adrenal energies, a sort of syringe on wheels. "We Build Excitement," in the words of Pontiac's slogan. The form of the commercial built a particular brand of excite-ment. In the case of the futuristic Dodge, the relentless flickering pace, the high-gloss platinum look, the glacially blue coloration, the dark ice haze, the metallic music innocent of wood and strings—all suggested something otherworldly and ungrounded. . . . The aggregate message was not about cars alone, but about the current incarnations of Amer-ica's perennial dreams: freedom, power, technology.

Gitlin suggests that car ads do not sell simply cars but also an ideology that prizes independence to the point of isolation, that links technology to a kind of cowboy masculinity. The aim of the Dodge ad is to make the viewer feel that Pontiac's cars are somehow more virile, edgy, and stylish than those of its competitors; Gitlin's aim is to connect this pitch to an American ethic that links violence to progress. And so many of his phrasings look two ways, toward both the advertisement and his reading of it. He describes the protagonist as both "handsome" and "robotic," "troubled" and "liberated," "awed" and yet, by the end of the spot, satisfied, grinning, "in the driver's seat." The streets are "evacuated" and yet, in an ethereal and blue-black way, alluring, vaporous, pulsing. And the car is the "active agent," teasing, pursuing, hypernew, transforming. In Gitlin's description, that is, the Dodge ad comes to reflect the "urgent and displaced velocity" of our culture.

What Gitlin has done is to give himself and his readers an example to use in thinking through some ideas about our common culture. The Dodge ad, that is, now serves a point that *he* is making. The aim of his writing is less to understand the commercial on its own terms than to use it as a way of getting at a larger issue in our culture. The text is not the object of his analysis so much as a tool for his thinking.

None of this is to suggest that you should be anything less than scrupulous in dealing with texts that you bring forward as illustrations in your writing. In formal academic writing, you need to cite nonprint media along with print texts—usually noting the site and date of a performance or broadcast, or when and how you accessed a website. Never work from memory alone. Always have copies of any texts you discuss at hand: not only books and magazines but videotapes, audiotapes, CDs, DVDs, MP3s, scripts, lyric sheets, printouts, Xeroxes, postcards, photographs, and so on.

Intertexts

Most research handbooks now include guides to citing nonprint media. Janice R. Walker and Todd Taylor's *Columbia Guide to Online Style* (New York: Columbia University Press, 1998) is especially helpful in offering not only rules but working principles for documenting texts in various media.

Take notes on interviews and events. If you can, try to reproduce some part of the texts you discuss in your writing. (It is easy enough to scan images into a text or even simply to paste in photos or Xeroxes, and it is quickly becoming more practicable to insert audio and visual files into electronic documents.) Save all the texts you write about, especially any that readers might have difficulties accessing on their own (web links get pulled down or changed, TV programs go off air, song lyrics can be unintelligible). The more confidence your readers have in your descriptions of such texts, the more they are also likely to credit your uses and interpretations of them.

Gitlin models a use of forwarding as a kind of opening move, a way into a subject. While this sort of move is not always made at the start of an essay or book, it does tend to mark hinge points in a text, moments where a writer is moving from one line of thought to another. Sometimes a writer may use a series of forwarded passages to stand for the key moves of a piece, to offer a kind of outline of it through images and examples. For instance, in the opening chapter of his book *On Literacy,* Robert Pattison defines literacy as involving not simply a mechanical mastery of the skills of reading and writing but also "a consciousness of the uses of languages." The literate person, Pattison suggests, realizes that words never simply describe the world but rather always offer a particular view of it, and thus that we can use language to shape beliefs and events—for both good and ill. He then argues that this awareness of the power of words to influence action is

> so fundamental that we may wonder if it is possible to be human without it. Three instances of this basic sort of illiteracy come to mind: the Wild Boy of Aveyron, Gracie Allen, and Homer's Agamemnon.

Pattison then structures the rest of his chapter around these three examples of illiteracy. The Wild Boy, as portrayed in Francois Truffaut's film, is someone who has grown up without ever learning to use language at all; the comedienne Gracie Allen, in her radio skits with Fred Burns, is a person who understands only the literal meaning of words, who never gets the joke or the pun; and Agamemnon, the leader of the Greek campaign against Troy in the *Iliad,* is a blustering bureaucrat who follows all the rules without question or criticism. While his argument is too involved to restate in detail, I think you can see how Pattison uses these examples to suggest the progress of his thought—moving from examples of individuals with no language to mistaken language

Intertexts

Robert Pattison, *On Literacy* (New York: Oxford University Press, 1982), 5–18.

to a competent but limited language. The Wild Boy, Gracie, and Agamemnon serve as markers of his ideas, steps in his argument, ways of thinking about his subject.

Authorizing

But texts are sources of terms and ideas as well as images and examples. A defining move of critical writing is the turn to another text for a key word or concept. Sometimes this occurs as a quick appeal to another writer as a voice of authority. For instance, in "Sex, Lies, and Advertising," Gloria Steinem invokes the views of an industry expert to support her claim that advertisers often exert an undue influence on the editorial content of the articles in women's magazines:

> Do you think, as I once did, that advertisers make decisions based on solid research? Well, think again. "Broadly speaking," says Joseph Smith of Octoby-Smith, Inc., a consumer research firm, "there is no persuasive evidence that the editorial context of an ad matters.

There is real wit to this brief citation, as Steinem in effect calls on her opponents in the advertising world to make her point for her. (Her essay was written to explain and defend the politically brave but economically risky decision of *Ms.* magazine to no longer accept advertising.) But Steinem's appeal to authority here is essentially the same as that made in the "review of the literature" sections of many academic essays and books, where we are diligently told "what research shows" or "what critics have observed" or the like. This sort of move is often necessary to make, if only to prove that you've done your homework, but it seems to me, for the most part, to be a straightforward and routine form of intellectual housekeeping. The best advice I can offer, then, is to follow Steinem's lead in making such appeals as succinct and pointed as you can. (Often they can be relegated to footnotes.)

Intertexts

Gloria Steinem, "Sex, Lies, and Advertising," *Ms.*, July–August 1990, 18–28; reprinted in Harris, Rosen, and Calpas, *Media Journal*, 436–55.

Borrowing

You can call on other texts not simply to support but to advance your work as writer through *borrowing* a term or idea from another writer to use in thinking through your subject. For instance, in *Amusing Ourselves to Death*, Neil Postman argues that we have shifted from a print- to a television-based culture, and in doing so have also begun to privilege entertainment and diversion over analysis. To explain what he feels is the dominant role that TV plays in our lives, Postman both contrasts it to another technology and draws on the work of a quite different writer and thinker:

> In the past few years, we have been learning that the computer is the technology of the future. We are told that our children will fail in school and be left behind in life if they are not "computer literate." We are told that we cannot run our businesses, or compile our shopping lists, or keep our checkbooks tidy unless we own a computer. Perhaps some of this is true. But the most important fact about computers and what they mean to our lives is that we learn about all this from television. Television has achieved the status of a "meta-medium"—an instrument that directs not only our knowledge of the world but our knowledge of *ways of knowing* as well.
>
> At the same time, television has achieved the status of "myth," as Roland Barthes uses the word. He means by *myth* a way of understanding the world that is not problematic, that we are not fully conscious of, that seems, in a word, natural. A myth is a way of thinking so deeply embedded in our consciousness that it is invisible. That is now the way of television. We are no longer fascinated or perplexed by its machinery. We do not tell stories of its wonders. We do not confine our television sets to special rooms.

Of course, anything written about computers is likely to seem comically out of date in little more than a year or two, and certainly, writing in 1985, Postman was not in a position to guess at the impact that computers, email, and the web would soon exert on our culture. But his point that computers continue to intrigue and trouble us while the technology of television seems natural and invisible, a simple and given presence, is still worth considering. Postman

---

Intertexts

Neil Postman, *Amusing Ourselves to Death* (New York: Viking, 1985), 78–79.

Postman is drawing on the preface to a collection of essays by Roland Barthes, *Mythologies*, trans. Annette Lavers (New York: Hill & Wang, 1972).

argues for this contrast by suggesting that television now functions as a kind of *myth*, "as Roland Barthes uses the word." That tag phrase is crucial to understanding what Postman is doing as a writer. Barthes was a French literary theorist who wrote from the 1950s through the 1970s and was one of the first serious critics of popular culture. But while he wrote occasionally on television, it was not one of his central interests. And, unlike Postman, Barthes wrote not only as a critic but as a fan of popular culture. What Postman takes from Barthes, then, is less an overall approach to looking at culture than a term and concept ("myth") that he finds useful for his own purposes. He does not "apply" Barthes to an analysis of television so much as *borrow* the idea of myth from him to explain how TV has now become natural and familiar to us. And then, having given thanks where due, Postman can, in a sense, return the term to Barthes with its original meaning more or less intact.

This quick, tactical use of other texts is one of the key moves of intellectual writing. To draw on the idea of myth, Postman doesn't need to come to terms with Barthes's overall project as a writer. He simply has to be clear about where the concept comes from and what he wants to do with it. In citing Barthes, does Postman enter into conversation with him? Not in any meaningful sense, it seems to me. Rather, he borrows and reuses materials made available by Barthes—and which I have then myself put to use here yet again. Plato worried that writing would allow texts to "roll about . . . indiscriminately," ungoverned by the aims of their authors and eventually falling into the hands of "those who have no business" with them. But the other side of this fear is the democratic hope that all of us can gain access to the materials of our culture and reshape them to our own purposes.

Extending

Indeed, I'd argue that writing tends to become more exciting as it moves outward—selecting, excerpting, commenting, and, sometimes, changing or inflecting the meanings of the texts it brings forward. Consider, for instance, another use of the work of Roland Barthes by a writer on television—in this case, David Marc in his book *Demographic Vistas,* an argument for the TV sitcom as a form of populist art:

"The virtue of [professional] wrestling," Roland Barthes wrote in 1957, "is that it is the spectacle of excess." The sitcom, in contrast, is a spectacle of subtleties, an incremental construction of substitute universes laid upon the foundation of a linear, didactic teletheater. Even the occasional insertion of the *mirabile* or supernatural underlines the genre's broader commitment to naturalistic imitation. Presentational comedy, which shared the prime-time spotlight with the sitcom during the early years of TV, vacillates between the danger of excess and the safety of consensus. The comedy-variety genre has been the great showcase for presentational teleforms: stand-up comedy, impersonation, and the blackout sketch. It is similar to wrestling, in that it too strives for the spectacle of excess. The pre-electronic ancestors of the comedy-variety show can be found on the vaudeville and burlesque stages. . . . But the comedy-variety show does not go to the ultimate excesses of wrestling. Like the sitcom, it is framed by the proscenium arch and accepts the badge of artifice.

Unlike Postman, who calls on the concept of myth "as Roland Barthes uses the word," Marc revises Barthes's phrasing almost in the act of quoting it. "The spectacle of excess" was how Barthes explained the allure of professional wrestling, describing its matches as mock, exaggerated battles between good and evil that fans can at once laugh at and revel in. (While Barthes wrote about wrestling in the 1950s, his words still describe much of the appeal of the WWF today.) In forwarding the idea of a "spectacle of subtleties," Marc puts his own spin on this celebration of the popular, arguing that the roots of the sitcom lie not in the excesses of burlesque or wrestling but in the nuances of domestic drama. To understand the sitcom, he suggests, you need a slightly different sense of spectacle. His aim is not to criticize Barthes's phrasing (which describes wrestling perfectly well) but to add to its range of meanings. In thus *extending* the notion of spectacle, Marc can at once link his position to Barthes and push beyond him. He quotes with a difference, turning Barthes's concept, in a move as

> **Intertexts**
>
> David Marc, *Demographic Vistas* (Philadelphia: University of Pennsylvania Press, 1984).
>
> Marc cites here the famous lead essay of Barthes's *Mythologies*, "The World of Wrestling," 15–25.

Intertexts

Marjorie Garber, "Our Genius Problem," *Atlantic Monthly*, December 2002, 67.

powerful as it is efficient, into one of his own.

If the stylistic signature of borrowing from another text is the note of acknowledgment ("in the words of *x*," "as *y* suggests," "as *z* uses the term"), then the characteristic marker of extending is the punning echo or substituted term—as shown, for instance, in Marc's rephrasing of the "spectacle of excess" as a "spectacle of subtleties." You can see the critic Marjorie Garber making both moves—acknowledgment and substitution—in the following passage from her essay "Our Genius Problem":

> Joseph Addison's essay "On Genius," published in *The Spectator* in 1711, laid out the terrain of genius as we use the term today, to denote exceptional talent or someone who possesses it. According to Addison, there were two kinds of genius—natural and learned . . . In general terms this dichotomy—brilliant vs. industrious—still underlies our notion of genius today, but despite Thomas Edison's oft quoted adage, "Genius is one percent inspiration and ninety-nine percent perspiration," it's the inspiration that we dote on.

Garber takes pains here to point out that her key descriptive words for genius come from Addison ("natural and learned") and Edison ("inspiration and perspiration"), gracefully noting how one "laid out the terrain" and how the other gave us his "oft quoted adage." But to connect their phrasings to each other, Garber needs to come up with a new dichotomy of her own—"brilliant vs. industrious"—which she slides adeptly between long dashes in her last sentence. This opposition echoes the form of the writers she quotes, but shifts some of their terms—replacing "natural" and "inspiration" with her own *"brilliant,"* and "learned" and "perspiration" with her *"industrious."* The result is a phrasing that draws on Addison and Edison, but that allows Garber to point out what now seems obvious: We expect our geniuses to be not simply dutiful and hardworking but brilliant. She does not simply restate but rewrites their familiar contrast in a way that lets her point out how one of its sides ("brilliant") tends to be favored over the other ("industrious"). Through forwarding Addison and Edison, she arrives at her own, separate position as a writer.

Projects

Defining Forwarding

Locate a text whose writer forwards the work of another intellectual or artist. See if the terms I have offered in this chapter are helpful in describing the uses the writer makes of this text. That is, does he forward the other text to *illustrate* a point he is making? Or does he cite it to *authorize* his claims? Or *borrow* or *extend* some of its ideas and phrasings? Or—and this is what would lend this project some real interest—do you see any points in the text where you would need a different term to name what the writer is doing? See if you can take the opportunity here, that is, to extend my vocabulary, to add to or revise the set of terms I have used to describe forwarding.

Some Complexities of Practice

In this chapter I've identified four types of forwarding: *illustrating, authorizing, borrowing,* and *extending.* A problem with offering advice about writing, though, is that while you can isolate certain moves that writers make, they rarely make those moves in isolation. In the course of an ambitious piece of writing, you are likely to forward the work of others in multiple and overlapping ways: to call on some texts as sources of authority, to draw on others for examples, to borrow ideas or extend phrasings from still others. And this does not even begin to consider the ways in which you will also probably need in the same piece to come to terms with or counter yet other texts. The thing to remember is that the strategies I describe in this book are just that: strategies, moves, ways of advancing your own project as a writer. In order to identify these strategies, I have chosen passages that show a writer making a certain move particularly well: Gitlin illustrating, Postman borrowing, Marc extending, and the like. But strong writers tend to use such moves in combination. In closing this chapter, then, I'd like to look briefly at a writer making use of several different strategies of forwarding all at once.

In *Fear of Falling,* the cultural critic Barbara Ehrenreich explores the anxious social and economic position of the professional middle class— teachers, writers, lawyers, doctors, engineers, administrators, and the like. Ehrenreich argues that because the members of this class realize that their position in society rests on their knowledge or expertise, they tend to be nervous about crediting the views of other, less-credentialed people.

> We tend to think of the problem, if we think of it at all, as a simple *lack* on the part of the "lower" classes, most likely a simple lack of vocabulary. Stereotypes of verbally deprived workers come to mind: Archie Bunker with his malapropisms, Ed Norton braying numbly on *The Honeymooners.* But usually it is the middle class that is speaking the strange language—something sociologist Alvin Gouldner called "critical discourse." This is the language of the academy and also of bureaucracy; and, in his analysis, it defines the professional middle class as a "speech community." It is distinguished, above all, by its impersonal and seemingly universal tone. Within critical discourse, Gouldner writes,
>
> > Persons and their social positions must not be visible in their speech. Speech becomes impersonal. Speakers hide behind their speech. Speech seems to be disembodied, de-contextualized and self-grounded.
>
> Relative to the vernacular, critical discourse operates at a high level of abstraction, always seeking to absorb the particular into the general, the personal into the impersonal. This is its strength. But the rudely undemocratic consequence is that individual statements from "below" come to seem almost weightless, fragmentary, unprocessed. . . . The way across the language barrier lies, first, through awareness of the middle-class assumptions that automatically denigrate "ordinary" styles of speech. In the longer term, we need a critique of critical discourse itself. Is there a way to "re-embody" the middle-class's impersonal mode of discourse, so that it no longer serves to conceal the individual and variable speaker? For we may

Intertexts

Barbara Ehrenreich, *Fear of Falling: The Inner Life of the Middle Class* (New York: Harper, 1989), 258–59. Ehrenreich quotes from Alvin Gouldner, *The Future of Intellectuals and the New Class* (New York: Seabury, 1979), 29.

need to find our*selves* in the language of abstraction, if we are ever to find the "others" in the language of daily life.

This seems to me an example of intellectual writing at its finest. The key move that Ehrenreich makes is to borrow the notion of critical discourse from Gouldner in order to suggest that it is not the working class but the middle class that is "speaking the strange language"—to reinterpret what at first seemed a "lack" of articulateness as simply a difference in styles of speech. But she also brings forward two TV texts—*All in the Family* and *The Honeymooners*—as quick illustrations of this seeming inarticulateness, and she deftly establishes the authority of Gouldner as a sociologist whose comments about middle-class speech are based on something more than opinion. But what I find most impressive is how she extends Gouldner's thinking through echoing and reworking his key terms. The problem with critical discourse, Ehrenreich suggests, is that it is not self-critical enough: "[W]e need a critique of critical discourse itself," she argues. Speech that Gouldner describes as "disembodied" she urges us to "re-embody." If middle-class "[s]peakers hide behind their speech," she exhorts us to "find our*selves* in" our language once again. Gouldner was trying to define the discourse of a particular middle-class community, what he called the "new class" of intellectuals. Ehrenreich wants us to recognize that community and its particular style of discourse so we can then push at its limits and constraints, to rethink the assumptions we bring to our attempts to listen to the speech of others. She brings pressure on Gouldner's ideas about critical discourse at the same time she draws upon them. In doing so, she shows how you can offer readers a new way of thinking about a text through the ways you rewrite its central terms and concepts.

Extending another text can be risky work. There is always the chance that you'll go too far, misappropriate the ideas or phrasings of another writer. Is a *spectacle of subtleties* really very much like a *spectacle of excess,* you might ask David Marc? Or do *learned* and *industrious* describe quite the same thing, you might ask Marjorie Garber? But I also think it is precisely the willingness to take such chances, to rewrite the terms and ideas of others, to make them your own, that so often makes extending such a salient move in ambitious intellectual prose.

Still, I want to be careful not to denigrate the other forms of forwarding. Citing authorities, culling examples, borrowing concepts or phrasings—these are moves you need to be able to make with confidence and speed. I also want to note that throughout this chapter, I have deliberately focused on the local and tactical—on ways to make use of specific images, phrasings, and concepts from other texts. There are broader ways of working in the mode of another writer, of taking on not just an idea or a term but an approach or perspective, a sensibility or method. I will discuss these moves in chapter 4 on *taking an approach.*

Before doing so, though, I will turn in the next chapter to a more critical and skeptical form of rewriting in which you aim to *counter* the positions taken by other writers, to note the limits of their work. In closing here, then, let me point to a shift in tone or style between forwarding and countering. In forwarding words, ideas, or images from another text, your focus tends to be on where you are headed as a writer, on what you're doing with your materials. But to counter another text effectively your focus usually needs to stay longer on its claims and phrasings. In a peculiar way, then, the act of countering or criticizing a text often lends it a stature that forwarding does not. You can imagine, for instance, David Marc deciding he needed to explain more fully the problems with looking at popular culture as a "spectacle of excess." But to do so he'd need to write a passage not on the sitcom and his ideas about it but on Roland Barthes. The work of countering a text tends to be slow and careful. The pace of forwarding is usually quicker, its touch lighter. Its aim is to take what is useful from a text and move on.

Projects

Forwarding Nonprint Texts

The next time you write an essay in which you discuss a nonprint text, try to find a way to incorporate that text as seamlessly as you can into your document. You might consider scanning images into the body of your text or embedding web links to audio or visual files in an electronic document. Or, if you don't have access to a scanner or web technology, you can still cut and paste images (ads, postcards, photos, etc.) into the text you are composing. See if you can "wrap" your text around the image (as my prose wraps around the inserts in this book). Xeroxing a page can make the interface between image and text appear more seamless. In any case, do not simply append images or links to the end of your text. Your goal should be instead to make those texts part of your own document.

I offer this project as both a technical *and* intellectual challenge. For I think you will find that once you insert an image (or other media text) into the body of your writing, you will feel a need to comment on it in ways that you might not have had you simply paper-clipped it to the back of your essay. Indeed, if you want to take this project a step further, see if you can quote the same nonprint text a second time in your essay, but isolating a particular aspect or fragment of it—a section of an image, perhaps, or a line from a scene, or a riff from a song. Experiment if you can with re-presenting or reformatting the text—through changing its shape, color, volume, and so on. Try not simply to reproduce the text but to forward it, to use it to make a point of your own.

3

Countering

Palin: Oh look, this isn't an argument.

Cleese: Yes it is.

Palin: No it isn't. It's just contradiction.

Cleese: No it isn't.

Palin: It is!

Cleese: It is not.

Palin: Look, you just contradicted me.

Cleese: I did not.

Palin: Oh you did!

Cleese: No, no, no.

Palin: You did just then.

Cleese: Nonsense!

Palin: Oh, this is futile!

Cleese: No it isn't.

Palin: I came here for a good argument.

Cleese: No you didn't; you came here for an argument.

Palin: An argument isn't just contradiction.

Cleese: It can be.

Palin: No it can't. An argument is a connected series of statements intended to establish a proposition.

Cleese: No it isn't.

Palin: Yes it is! It's not just contradiction.

Cleese: Look, if I argue with you, I must take up a contrary position.

Palin: Yes, but that's not just saying, "No it isn't."

Cleese: Yes it is!

Palin: No it isn't! Argument is an intellectual process. Contradiction is just the automatic gainsaying of any statement the other person makes.

(short pause)

Cleese: No it isn't.

—Monty Python, "Argument Clinic"

Always, no sometimes, think it's me
But you know I know when it's a dream
I think I know I mean a "Yes" but it's all wrong
That is I think I disagree.

—John Lennon and Paul McCartney,
"Strawberry Fields Forever"

I recall writing an essay in graduate school in which I did everything I could to rebut the views of a certain scholar. I was determined to prove my opponent wrong, and I seized upon every gap, contradiction, or misstep that I could find in his text in order to do so. After reading my essay, my professor evidently agreed that I had won the imaginary debate I had set up, since he made no effort to find fault with my argument or examples. But rather than congratulating me, as I had expected and hoped, he asked instead: "Why are you spending so much time discussing the work of somebody you seem to think isn't very bright?"

I often think back to that moment when I find myself locked in argument with a text that I am trying to write about. The question I've learned to ask myself at such times is: What do I hope will result from pursuing this disagreement? If the answer is simply that I think I can prove that the text I am reading has certain shortcomings or limits, then I try to set aside the temptation to argue. All texts have their moments of blindness. Simply to note them is to do little. But if I can use certain problems in a text as a springboard to get at something I couldn't otherwise say, to develop a line of thinking of my own, then I try to note those problems in a way that allows me to quickly move on to my own counterproposals or ideas.

Or, to put this another way, the aim of academic writing should not be simply to prove how smart you are but to add to what can be said about a subject. To do so, you may sometimes need to identify the weaknesses or limits of other writings, but that shouldn't be the sole point of your writing. Critique needs to lead to alternatives. Correcting the ideas of another writer may seem an intuitive way of rewriting their work—you identify what they've gotten wrong and then you show them how to get it right—but the sort of countering I want to talk about in this chapter differs from such verbal swordplay. As I use the term, to *counter* is not to nullify but to suggest a different way of thinking. Its defining phrases are *On the other hand . . .* and *Yes, but . . .* (In contrast, the defining phrase of forwarding is *Yes, and . . .*) Countering looks at other views and texts not as wrong but as *partial*—in the sense of being both interested and incomplete. In countering you bring a different set of interests to bear upon a subject, look to notice what others have not. Your aim is not to refute what has been said before, to bring the discussion to an end, but to respond to prior views in ways that move the conversation in new directions.

Projects

The Tone of Countering

Find two texts that counter the work of other writers but that strike you as doing so with differing degrees of civility. That is, see if you can locate one text whose writer articulates her or his differences with other intellectuals clearly but with a sense of restraint or good humor, and another whose writer seems more overly antagonistic toward the work he is responding to. Try to point to specific moments or moves in the two texts that help account for their differences in tone.

This is not to suggest that academic writers disagree with one another in especially muted or polite ways. On the contrary, they often state their differences in quite clear and forceful terms. But what distinguishes the practice of countering is that it pushes beyond mere disagreement. Popular debates tend to begin with their conclusions. That is, a speaker is identified from the start as holding a specific, already formulated position—as being for or against capital punishment or tax cuts or gay marriage or whatever—and then everything she or he goes on to say is understood as either defending that position or attacking the opposing view. But the aim of countering is to open up new lines of inquiry. The questions to ask of a writer countering another text thus have less to do with decorum than use. If all you really want to do is to show how someone else is wrong, then it doesn't much matter how politely you phrase your criticisms. But if it is clear that your own writing in some real sense depends upon the text you are countering, that your own position has evolved in response to its ideas and phrasings, then your readers (if not always the author of the text you are discussing) are more likely to see your criticisms of it as fair and useful.

Since the aim of countering is to develop a new line of thinking in response to the limits of other texts, it almost always involves a close attention to the specifics of their structure and phrasing. In countering the work of another writer, then, you usually need first to come to terms with his or her project, to offer a sense of its aims and strengths. To identify what a text fails to do, you need to be clear about what it achieves—or at least what it attempts. Otherwise your criticisms will seem flippant or unearned. But even the most civil of criticisms can sting. There is an unavoidable adversarial edge to countering, as you seek less to connect your views with those of the texts you are reading than to separate them. Forwarding aligns; countering individuates. I see three main ways of creating this sort of critical distance:

- *Arguing the other side:* Showing the usefulness of a term or idea that a writer has criticized or noting problems with one that she or he has argued for.
- *Uncovering values:* Surfacing a word or concept for analysis that a text has left undefined or unexamined.
- *Dissenting:* Identifying a shared line of thought on an issue in order to note its limits.

All three of these moves can be easier to make with force than grace. It is hard to differ in a pleasing or civil way. The only real way to do so, it seems to me, is to show as clearly as you can how noting the limits of a text has led you to a new line of work or inquiry. In that sense, the key moment in a counterstatement is when it stops, when a writer turns from the text he is reading in order to offer a proposal of his own. Let me turn to a number of examples of how writers can set up such points of divergence, of new lines of thought emerging from old ones.

Arguing the Other Side

In his celebrated series of essays on *Ways of Seeing,* John Berger shows how we can look at oil paintings in ways that focus not only on their artistic form or technique but also on the content of their images—that is, on the people and things that these paintings represent. Berger argues that an exclusive attention to form obscures much of what paintings can tell us about how people lived in the past, not only in terms of their material surroundings but also their social relationships—how they wished to be seen by others and how others actually viewed them. This view puts him at odds with many art historians and critics. For instance, in discussing how women are portrayed in oil paintings, Berger takes on the work of Kenneth Clark, a distinguished writer on the history of art.

> We can now begin to see the difference between nakedness and nudity in the European tradition. In his book on *The Nude* Kenneth Clark maintains that to be naked is simply to be without clothes, whereas the nude is a form of art. According to him, the nude is not the starting point of a way of a painting, but a way of seeing which the painting achieves. To some degree, this is true—although the way of seeing "a nude" is not necessarily confined to art: there are also nude photographs, nude poses, nude gestures. What is true is that the nude is always conventionalized—and the authority for its conventions derives from a certain tradition of art.
>
> What do these conventions mean? What does a nude signify? It is not sufficient to answer these questions merely in terms of the art-form, for it is quite clear that the nude also relates to lived sexuality.

Intertexts

John Berger, *Ways of Seeing,* (New York: Penguin, 1977), 53–54. This book was based on a series of programs broadcast on the BBC and has been reprinted over twenty times.

Berger is responding to Kenneth Clark, *The Nude* (Princeton: Princeton University Press, 1972).

To be naked is to be oneself.

To be nude is to be seen naked by others and yet not recognized for oneself. A naked body has to be seen as an object in order to become a nude. (The sight of it as an object stimulates the use of it as an object.) Nakedness reveals itself. Nudity is placed on display.

To be naked is to be without disguise.

To be on display is to have the surfaces of one's own skin, the hairs of one's own body, turned into a disguise which, in that situation, can never be discarded. The nude is condemned to never being naked. Nudity is a form of dress.

Projects

Reading Visual Culture

Read through the essays in *Ways of Seeing* with the aim of better understanding how Berger makes use of visual texts in his writing. How useful are the terms I offer in this book in accounting for how he cites, describes, and comments on the images in his book? How might you draw on his work to revise and expand the vocabulary of rewriting that I propose here?

I need to note that in simply quoting Berger's prose here I am slighting one of the most remarkable aspects of *Ways of Seeing,* which is his interspersing of images throughout his text not simply to illustrate but to advance his thinking. (In this instance the first paragraph I've quoted is framed, top and bottom, by images of Eastern erotica and by softcore photos of nude models from a men's magazine.) But my interest here centers on how Berger inverts Clark's distinction between the naked and the nude. He begins by rehearsing what Clark has to say about their differences: "to be naked is simply to be without clothes, whereas the nude is a form of art." He then grudgingly admits that there is something to this distinction, at least in the sense that the nude is always a conventionalized way of seeing. But he then quickly raises some points that Clark doesn't consider—that the conventions of the nude are not confined to the higher realms of art but are also part of the vernacular of erotica, of "nude photographs, nude poses, nude gestures," and, more important, that nakedness and nudity refer not just to painting but to the lived experiences of individuals. And in life rather than art, Berger argues, nakedness has a value that nudity does not. To be naked is to be at home in your own skin; to be nude is to pose for the gaze of another.

Berger thus offers here an unusually clear illustration of *arguing the other side*—attaching a positive value to something another writer denigrates or a negative value to what another writer applauds. In this case, Kenneth Clark sees the nude as an artistic achievement and nakedness as merely banal, while for Berger nakedness represents authentic sexuality and the nude its conventionalized packaging. The values attached to the two terms are flipped. But note how Berger suggests that Clark is not so much wrong as incomplete, unaware of the full implications of the distinction he is making. He agrees with Clark that the nude is a conventionalized form of seeing, but he also counters that what may sometimes be good for art is not always good for living. His critique thus does not simply cancel out what Clark as to say but rather adds to the ways we can think about the ways bodies are represented in art.

Uncovering Values

In a way, Clark does Berger a favor in so clearly opposing the naked and the nude—since Berger is then able to use Clark's own terms of analysis in countering his work. He simply needs to flip the terms of a distinction that Clark has already made for him. But you will often find that you need to *uncover* a term of value that a text has obscured or repressed before you can question it. For instance, in her book on the masculine ethos of cyberculture, *Cracking the Gender Code*, Melanie Stewart Millar looks at the image of the digital generation offered by the cover of *Wired* magazine.

It is useful to once again compare *Wired* with a more familiar and ubiquitous magazine genre, the women's fashion magazine.

> **Intertexts**
>
> Melanie Stewart Millar, *Cracking the Gender Code: Who Rules the Wired World?* (Toronto: Sumach Press, 1998), 114–15.
> Millar refers to Ellen McCracken, *Decoding Women's Magazines* (New York: St. Martin's 1993).

According to Ellen McCracken's useful study of the genre, the cover model on a so-called women's magazine represents a "window to the future self," a symbol of what the reader can achieve by consuming the magazine's content. The cover of *Wired* magazine serves an analogous function as both the window to the individual reader's future and to a more generalized future world. The cover does more than simply catch the eye of the casual passerby. *Wired*'s cover graphic, which most often depicts a celebrity of the digital generation, challenges the (presumed) male reader to emulate the achievements of the cover "model," who is almost always a white male. Just as the cover model of *Cosmopolitan* comes to signify the "Cosmo girl," and all the values endorsed by the magazine, so the figure on *Wired* magazine represents elite members of the digital generation. And, like the model on the cover of a fashion magazine, the image on *Wired*'s cover plays on the vulnerabilities of its intended readers in order to draw them in. Female readers of fashion magazines find themselves drawn to the unrealistic, fantastic images of the current feminine ideal and the attendant promises of happiness and regeneration; so the digital generation sees on the cover of *Wired* magazine a graphic representation of all that they (apparently) want to be. While the fashion magazine promises to replace anxiety and empti- ness with the adulation that cosmetic beauty provides, *Wired* promises to replace a sense of lack of control or fear of emasculation with a rein- vigorated form of masculine privilege in a digital world.

Projects

Extending Millar

In countering *Wired,* Millar borrows an idea from Ellen McCracken's *Decoding Women's Magazines*—that of the magazine cover as a "window to the future self." Locate a copy of McCracken's book to see how she develops this approach. What are the strengths of this mode of reading? What are its limits? Are there things that the covers of popular magazines do besides present an idealized image of themselves to their readers? That is, how might you extend or counter Millar's and McCracken's view of how magazine covers seduce prospective readers?

Millar plays here with a distinction found not so much *in* the text of *Wired* as *around* it. It is as if she is reading *Wired* not in isolation but as it sits on a newsstand or supermarket rack, next to magazines whose covers feature, in one sense, the very same thing, the cover model as future self, and in another sense, something quite different: *women*. In showing how the "Wired man" is similar in many ways to the "Cosmo girl," she raises questions about why, in each case, the self of the future seems governed by stereotypes of the present. She uncovers a male/female binary underlying the cover images of *Wired* that associates technical progress with masculine sexuality. Unlike Berger, she does not argue for the devalued term in this binary; there is no case made here for the "Wired girl." Her aim is rather to call into question *Wired*'s implicit (and perhaps unconscious) linking of technology, power, and sexuality.

Millar's stance toward *Wired* is more unremittingly hostile than Berger's toward Clark. But while she is critical of the sexual politics of *Wired*, she acknowledges the power of its response to the "sense of lack of control or fear of emasculation" felt by its readers. She reads the cover of *Wired* as a sign of a larger problem in our culture in which technology is offered as an easy solution to anxieties whose actual sources are personal and political. In that sense she uses her critique of *Wired* to begin to develop new ways of thinking about the appeals and perils of digital culture.

Projects

Countering and Agonism

Perhaps the clearest place to see intellectual work at its most adversarial or antagonistic is in the "Letters to the Editor" or the "Comments and Response" sections of magazines and journals, since this is a site where writers often directly confront each other over the meaning or intent of their work—correcting inaccuracies, protesting misinterpretations, arguing politics, contesting reviews and uses of their writing.

Find an exchange between two writers in a "Letters" or "Response" section. (You will probably also want to look up the book, article, or review that prompted their interchange of views.) Read their letters in light of what I have said here about countering the work of others. To what degree do you see them employing the moves—reversing and uncovering terms of value, disputing consensus positions—that I discuss here? In what ways does their exchange or argument draw on different strategies and modes of response? What do you find interesting about their exchange? What, if anything, do you find troubling?

Our texts always say more than we mean. As writers we participate in the discourses of our culture in ways we can never fully control, and may not always be aware of. Rather, the values and attitudes of our society are often insinuated in the very metaphors and turns of phrase, examples and images, stories and characters, that we are given to work with in writing. And so while I doubt that the designers of *Wired* consciously intended to reinforce the masculine ethos of our culture, any more than the creators of the Dodge ad that Todd Gitlin talks about did, or than Sigmund Freud did in developing his theories of psychoanalysis—this doesn't mean that you can't look for signs of how their texts were (in part) shaped by the gendered attitudes of that culture. This is a frequent move in countering, the *uncovering* of values that, without being stated openly, undergird a text and influence what it says.

Such values are sometimes stated outright, at other times repressed, and at still others only hazily conceived. They often turn out to be connected to deep cultural beliefs about gender, race, sexuality, social class, and religion. But countering is not an exercise in political correctness; it is a move to examine what a text (or set of texts) leaves unmarked or unquestioned, to highlight the unseen. Noticing what is absent, what a certain text or approach fails to consider, is not an easy task, but it is a key move in writing criticism. One way of uncovering the values that drive a text is to ask what it appears *not* to find interesting. And so, for instance, John Berger reclaims the value of nakedness, which for Kenneth Clark seemed merely the mundane raw material of the nude; Carol Gilligan explores what Freud simply left unstudied as the "dark continent" of women's psychological development; and Melanie Stewart Millar reveals the "Cosmo girl" as the anxious alter ego of the "Wired man." Each critic illustrates how learning to notice what a text leaves unasked, or takes for granted, can offer you a powerful way of not only countering but also building upon its ideas.

Dissenting

As you will have noticed by this point, countering draws on many of the skills involved in coming to terms with texts that I discussed in chapter 1. You need to be able to represent the project of another writer, to identify key words and concepts from his text, to suggest its possible uses and strengths—so you can then pivot and show what the text leaves undone or how its terms might serve a different set of aims and interests. This move is made even more complex when your aim is to counter not just the work of a single writer but to dissent from a view shared by a number of thinkers. In such cases you need first to show that a certain consensus exists, so you can then define your position against it. Like a fruit cart on the set of a chase scene in a movie, you build it in order to knock it over.

One quick way of defining a shared approach to an issue is to list some of the key words in its vocabulary or to catalogue some of its central concepts. Recall, for instance, how Marjorie Garber deftly assembled shared definitions for "genius" from seemingly disparate authors. But while such an approach works well when you are trying to identify a loose *cluster* of concerns, you are likely to find at other times that you need to counter something more like a shared *line* of thought. What you need to do in such cases is to show how this line proceeds from one point to the next, to restate the key moves or logic of the argument in your own words—and then to offer examples of writers making these same moves. You are then in a position to counter the line of thinking you have defined.

There is a kind of template for many academic essays in which a writer says something like this: *Until now, writers on this subject have disagreed on points* a, b, *and* c. *However, underlying this disagreement, there is a consensus of views on point* d. *In this essay, I will show why point* d *is wrong.* Such a countering of an accepted position, of the common ground on which other disagreements rest, is shown brilliantly by the philosopher and critic

Alexander Nehamas in his essay "Serious Watching." In this piece Nehamas takes on the view held by many academics and intellectuals (like Neil Postman) that television is somehow an inferior medium to print. Here is how Nehamas sets up his argument:

> The common criticisms of television, though they are united in their disdain for the medium, come from various directions and have differing points. Wayne Booth, for example, expresses a relatively traditional preference for primarily linguistic over mainly visual works:
>
> > The video arts tell us precisely what we should see, but their resources are thin and cumbersome for stimulating our moral and philosophical range.
>
> A related criticism is made by John Cawelti, whose celebrated study of the arts of popular culture, particularly of formulaic literature, has led him to conclude that
>
> > formulaic works necessarily stress intense and immediate kinds of excitement and gratification as opposed to the more complete and ambiguous analyses of character and motivation that characterize mimetic literature.
>
> He also considers that a "major characteristic of formulaic literature is the dominant influence of the goals of escape and entertainment." The contrast here is one between the straightforward, action-oriented, and entertaining popular works which by and large belong to popular culture—works which include the products of television—and the ambiguous, innovative, psychologically motivated and edifying works of high art.
>
> Finally, Catherine Belsey, who has approached the study of literature from a Marxist point of view, following the work of Louis Althusser, draws a contrast between "classic realism, still the dominant popular mode in literature, film, and television" which is characterized by "illusionism, narrative which leads to closure, and a hierarchy of texts which establishes the 'truth' of the story" with what she calls "the interrogative text." . . . It would be easy to cite many other similar passages, but the main themes of the attack against television, to which those other passages would provide only variations, are all sounded by these three authors: (1) given its formulaic nature, television drama is simple and action-oriented; it makes few demands of its audience and offers them quick and shallow gratification; (2) given its visual,

nonlinguistic character, it is unsuited for providing psychological and philosophical depth; and (3) given its realist tendencies, it fails to make its own fictional nature one of its themes. . . . These reasons are taken to show that television does not deserve serious critical attention—or that, if it does, it should only be criticized on ideological grounds.

And yet there are reasons to be suspicious of this view, which can all be based on a serious look, for example, at *St. Elsewhere*—a television drama that appears straightforward, action-oriented, and realistic.

Nehamas then goes on to offer a close reading of the 1980s series *St. Elsewhere*, a program that blended the conventions of realistic drama and ironic farce in ways that many viewers found alternately moving and hilarious. Nehamas argues that such programs demonstrate that television can well repay "serious watching," that psychological depth and artistic innovation are not solely the properties of the medium of print. What interests me here, though, is how hard Nehamas works to show that he is not arguing against a straw man, but that there is in fact a widespread "disdain" toward TV shared by most intellectuals.

Nehamas's argument is unusually complex and involved—in large part because he is dealing with not one but several writers. In grouping and responding to the critics of TV, Nehamas makes a number of moves that are worth noting and imitating. First, he offers a diverse set of figures who endorse a negative view of TV—citing a traditional humanist, a writer on popular culture, and a Marxist critic (all of whom he is careful to identify as such). These are not the sorts of thinkers whom you might expect to agree on many issues, and so when Nehamas can show each of them expressing the same attitude of impatience with

> ## Intertexts
>
> Alexander Nehamas, "Serious Watching," *South Atlantic Quarterly* 89 (Winter 1990); reprinted in Joseph Harris, Jay Rosen, and Gary Calpas, eds., *Media Journal: Reading and Writing about Popular Culture*, 2nd ed. (Boston: Allyn & Bacon, 1999), 320–36.
>
> In the interest of concision, I have edited the passages Nehamas quotes, along with some of his own prose. The critics he cites are:
>
> Wayne Booth, "The Company We Keep: Self-Making in Imaginative Art," *Daedalus* 111 (Fall 1982).
>
> John Cawelti, *Adventure, Mystery, and Romance* (Chicago: University of Chicago Press, 1976).
>
> Catherine Belsey, *Critical Practice* (London: Verso, 1980).

the seemingly formulaic nature of TV, then his claim that this is a common view seems reasonable. (And while there is of course no magic number of examples needed to prove such a case, three seems just enough to quickly suggest a trend.) Second, Nehamas quotes from these critics in a way that allows him to associate the stance he is describing with a series of key opposing terms: Television is thin, formulaic, escapist, illusionist; high art is philosophical, complex, interrogative. He is then able to echo these terms and values in his own summary of the antitelevision position (in the next-to-last paragraph). Finally, this groundwork allows him, much like Berger, to argue the other side, to use the words of Booth, Cawelti, Belsey, et al. in pointing out the problems of their position. You can see the beginnings of this reversal in the last paragraph I've quoted, in which Nehamas tells us that he will now turn to look seriously at a television text that "*appears* straightforward, action-oriented, and realistic" (my emphasis). It will probably not surprise you to learn that he reads *St. Elsewhere* instead as complex, absorbed in the intricacies of character, and reflective about its status as a fiction—as possessing, that is, all of the qualities of art as Booth, Cawelti, and Belsey define it. I say this not to suggest that the rest of his essay is routine but to point out how powerfully Nehamas's own position evolves in response to theirs. In rereading *St. Elsewhere,* Nehamas rewrites their stance on the boundaries between art and popular entertainment.

Civility

I have struggled in this chapter to define countering as a practice that differs from the sort of argument whose goal is simply to vanquish your opponent. I've suggested that coming to terms with another text is a necessary prelude to countering it, and have tried to show how the aim of countering should not be simply to note the gaps or limits of another text but to use that critique to develop a position of your own. And I have identified three tactics for doing so: *arguing the other side, uncovering values,* and *dissenting.* But even if you keep your focus as a writer less on the problems of a text than on the work you want to do with it, you still can't counter without disagreeing. There is a necessary agonism—a staking out of positions and differences— to much intellectual work. But behind texts and ideas lie people, and you want to be able to disagree about points of view without alienating the persons who hold them. I'd like to conclude this chapter, then, with some thoughts on the art of honest yet civil disagreement.

- *Focus on positions more than phrasings:* You need to attend to a writer's particular use of words in order to precisely note and counter the limits of his or her work. However, an unremitting focus on the wording of a text can often seem more hostile than scrupulous. The novelist Mary McCarthy is said to have remarked of her political and intellectual rival Lillian Hellman, "Every word she writes is a lie, including *and* and *the.*" The comment tells us far more about McCarthy than Hellman. You don't want to seem preoccupied with niceties of phrasing, with refuting every step or move made by a writer, as though nothing she might ever do could possibly please you. Your job is not to correct the infelicities of a text but to respond to and rework the position it puts forward. If you describe that position as mean-spirited or flimsy, as riddled with unfortunate phrasings and lying *ands* and *thes,* you are also likely to raise questions about your own motives in responding to it (as I learned back in grad school). But if you represent that position as a serious one, then your response is likely to seem the same as well. And so, in countering another writer, restate her or his project in clear and generous terms, quote just enough of her or his text to set up your response to it, and then move as quickly as you can from its language to your own.

- *Don't guess at intent:* It's tempting to imagine that people who disagree with you do so for sinister reasons. Maybe the guys at *Wired* did really just want, in the end, to be cooler than the jocks, to invent a new and improved form of machismo.

Or maybe the critics of TV really are just a bunch of snobs who refuse to like anything that ordinary people enjoy. Or maybe not. We'll never know, and in any case, it doesn't much matter. If the new image of manhood now has as much to do with technical prowess as muscle, then jokes about cyber-geeks miss the mark. If television really is incapable of conveying psychological nuance, then the snobs are right. In countering you need to respond to the position taken, not to the person taking it. Assume that other writers say what they have to say not out of an overweening desire for status or power, or because their thinking has been molded by their profession or class or gender, but because they genuinely find certain ideas compelling and useful. And then explain why you don't. Notice, for instance, how John Berger says very little about Kenneth Clark himself, but rather restates the distinction he draws between the naked and the nude, points out what that contrast accomplishes, and then turns it on its head, arguing for the value of nakedness. He offers a critique without picking a fight. This isn't to say that all aspects of the personal can be removed from intellectual disagreement. But what most often sparks anger is the questioning not of ideas but of motives.

- *Be careful with modifiers:* Don't use adjectives and adverbs to do your dirty work, to hint at a negative attitude toward a text or writer that you are reluctant to state more openly. What may seem throwaway terms can subtly but powerfully color an account of another writer's work: *clearly, simply, wholly, indeed, in fact, quite,* and so on. If it is *quite clear,* for instance, that there is a problem with a certain point of view, then it can seem as if it must have taken a willful obtuseness for other writers to have missed it. Be cautious, too, with terms of faint praise. I once read a response to an essay I had written that at various points described my work as "well-intentioned," "sincere," "reasonable," and "earnest" (although also, of course, completely mistaken; these are all terms invariably followed by a *but*). Now it's one thing to be called wrong, but being cast as a well-meaning but bumbling do-gooder struck me as an unkind—even if unintended—cut. Neither was it flattering to realize that the writer had evidently felt it necessary to assure readers that my approach in fact was not conniving, insincere, unreasonable, and duplicitous. The point is that small modifiers can play large roles in how your work gets read. You want the force of what you have to say to reside in your nouns and verbs, not in your descriptors. State both the strengths and limits of other positions as plainly as you can; in most cases, you will simply want to say that there are problems with a certain view, not that it is either "clearly mistaken" or "sincere but misguided."

- *Stress what you bring to the discussion:* The point of countering is to push knowledge forward. In the end, the readers of your text want to know what *you* have to tell them about the subject or issue at hand. I've suggested in this chapter that there are three steps to countering: coming to terms with another point of view, noting its limits, and constructing your own position in response. The emphasis of your writing should fall on that third step. An essay needs to be something more than simply a critique of the work of someone else. You need to have a point of your own to make, and you need to give yourself space to make it. While I don't want to reduce the notion of emphasis to a simple counting of lines or paragraphs, there's almost surely something wrong, for instance, with a six-page essay that consists of five pages of critique and only one of new thinking. The most civil way to counter another writer is to show how your response to her work opens up new forms of talk about her (and your) subject.

Some readers of this book have argued that the view I offer here of countering is idealized—that the goal of much academic writing really is to demonstrate a mastery over your materials and your rivals, to stake out a position and to defend it against attack. And, certainly, there is plenty of evidence for such a view. For instance, in *You Just Don't Understand*, her study of differing conversational styles, Deborah Tannen suggests that it is the pleasure that intellectuals take in the exchange of opposing views, in the give-and-take of open debate, that most distinguishes (and sometimes isolates) them from the rest of the culture. And in *Clueless in Academe*, itself an engaging brief for the life of the mind, Gerald Graff suggests that how to engage in a good argument is precisely what many university students (whose writing he feels is more likely to suffer from blandness than conten-

Intertexts

Gerald Graff, *Clueless in Academe: How Schooling Obscures the Life of the Mind* (New Haven: Yale University Press, 2003).

Deborah Tannen, *You Just Don't Understand: Women and Men in Conversation* (New York: Morrow, 1990).

tiousness) most need to learn. And I perhaps ought to acknowledge that I have not often been faulted myself for a reluctance to say what I think. But to admit that academic writing can often be adversarial is not to say that such writing is always *at its best* adversarial. I'm all for energetic and sharp prose that clarifies where a writer stands. But the sort of academic argument I most admire doesn't look all that much like argument in the familiar sense—since it aims less to offer reasons *behind* competing positions than to suggest what such differences might point *toward*. And so, for instance, in the passage I quote above, the point that Alexander Nehamas makes is not simply that he disagrees with the academic critics of television. Rather, he uses his differences with those writers to set up his own more appreciative reading of *St. Elsewhere* and popular culture. The critics of TV remain present in his prose even as he moves past them. That's the sort of intellectual work I'm trying to teach toward (and that I imagine Tannen and Graff teach as well). In arguing for civility, then, I'm not pressing for a mere politeness, but for a style of countering that doesn't stop at disagreement but instead pushes on for something more—that rewrites the work of others in order to say something new.

Projects

Skepticism and Civility

Go back through an essay you are currently working on and reread those passages where you deal with other texts. Make some notes regarding the stance or attitude you take toward their authors' work:

- What *use* do you make of the texts you cite? (You can either draw on the terms of this book or to invent your own.) How do these texts contribute to your own line of thinking? What phrases in your writing mark out this use?
- How would you describe your *attitude* toward the texts and writers you deal with? Angry? Superior? Respectful? Generous? Doubtful? Admiring? Noncommittal? What particular words or phrasings in your text suggest this stance? Ask yourself if your prose conveys the attitude toward these other texts and writers that you want it to.

Use your notes to consider how you might change or refine your use of other texts in your essay. The point here is to think about how you want to approach these texts on both *intellectual* and *stylistic* levels. There is no formula for how to do so. You can counter work that you respect and draw insights from texts that you find problematic. You can seem too aggressive, but you can also seem too dutiful. It's up to you to decide both what uses you want to make of other writers and how you want to be seen as approaching them.

4

Taking an Approach

. . . nothing of him that doth fade
But doth suffer a sea-change
Into something rich and strange.

        —William Shakespeare, *The Tempest*

It's the same old song
But with a different meaning
Since you've been gone.

        —Holland/Dozier/Holland, "It's the Same Old Song"

The various moves I've talked about so far in this book—*coming to terms, forwarding,* and *countering*—are ways of marking out your words and ideas from those of the texts you are working with. The very typography of academic writing speaks to this concern, with its use of quotation marks, text blocks, separate fonts, and notes to distinguish the separate voices that make up an essay. By noting what others have had to say on a subject, defining where their thinking ends and yours begins, you can make your own stance as a writer all the more clear. Indeed, a useful move in revising a critical essay is to go back through a draft and highlight where you quote or represent the work of others and where you develop your own line of argument. (See the Projects box "Tracking Influences" at the end of this chapter.) In doing so, you will often see the shape of a dialogue begin to appear in your writing, as you alternate between restating the views of others and responding to and making use of their work. In this chapter, however, I want to turn to a use of other texts that is harder to mark with precision but is nonetheless a key move in much intellectual writing—and that is working in the mode of another writer, or what I will call *taking an approach.*

There is a weak version of taking an approach in which one assumes the role of a disciple, adopting (rather than adapting) the moves and interests of another thinker. This often leads to a form of school writing with which you are no doubt familiar—the essay in which you are asked to *apply* the ideas of a writer to a certain subject, with the aim not so much of testing those ideas but of proving their validity. Almost any of the texts I've quoted in this book could serve as the basis for this sort of assignment: Apply your reading of John Berger to the depiction of women in fashion magazines. Or, apply your reading of Alexander Nehamas to another disdained medium—to comic books or musical shows or romance novels or whatever. And so on. When done in a routine fashion, such writing merely provides more examples of what has already been argued by Berger or Nehamas or whomever. Little new knowledge is created. Instead the disciple simply shows that the master is correct.

To make new knowledge your examples need to raise problems for your theory. It has to turn out, for instance, that the images of women in fashion magazines don't jibe entirely with the ideas of John Berger. And then as a writer you need to come up with some ideas of your own about both how to read those images and how to rewrite Berger in order to better account for them. When you take on the approach of another writer both your thinking and theirs need to change. Otherwise you are simply applying ideas to examples. To transform is to reshape, not to replace or rebut. The original does not go away but is remade into something new.

Such a reworking of materials goes on all the time in fiction, film,

> ## Intertexts
>
> Aretha Franklin, "Respect," *Natural Woman* (Atlantic, 1967).
>
> Herbie Hancock, Cantaloupe Island," *Empyrean Blues* (Blue Note, 1964).
>
> Jimi Hendrix, "Star-Spangled Banner," *Woodstock* (Atlantic, 1967).
>
> Bruce Hornsby, "The Way It Is," *The Way It Is* (RCA, 1986).
>
> Otis Redding, "Respect," *Otis Blue* (Atlantic, 1965).
>
> Tupac Shakur, "Changes," *2Pac's Greatest Hits* (Amaru/Deathrow/Interscope,1998).
>
> US3, "Flip Fantasia," *Hand on the Torch* (Blue Note, 1993).

and music. The cover song, in which one musician reinterprets a song associated with another, is a staple of rock and roll. And what you listen for in a good cover is not an imitation of the original, as in karaoke or *American Idol,* but a new rendering of it. Think of Aretha Franklin turning Otis Redding's macho demand for "Respect" into an assertion of female independence, or Jimi Hendrix interpreting the "Star-Spangled Banner" as an anthem of destruction. Hip-hop artists often sample and rework bits and phrases from other songs in similarly powerful and subtle ways: Consider, for instance, Tupac Shakur's angry and cynical quotation of Bruce Hornsby's "The Way It Is" in his own "Changes," or US3's homage to Herbie Hancock's jazz classic, "Cantaloupe Island," in their "Flip Fantasia."

Projects

Interpreting Cover Songs

Find two different recordings of the same song and listen to both carefully in order to consider how the *meaning* (and not just the feel or the style) of the cover version might be said to differ from that of the original.

To do so, you'll need first to make a specific list of the differences between the two versions in terms of lyrics, instrumentation, pace and rhythm, vocal emphasis, and the like. But then, and more important, you'll need to look for *patterns* in the changes between the cover and the original, so that you can then speculate on the perspective that lies beneath them.

Writers have similarly reworked old materials for centuries. The Greek dramas were based on stories well known to their audiences, and Shakespeare continually borrowed the plots of his plays from other sources. Current novelists continue this practice of reworking familiar stories. In *Mary Reilly,* for instance, Valerie Martin raises issues of gender and class in her retelling of the story of Jekyll and Hyde from the point of view of a maidservant working in Dr. Jekyll's house. Jean Rhys offers a new and dark subtext for *Jane Eyre* in

Intertexts

Jane Austen, *Emma* (1815; New York: Modern Library, 1980).

Emily Brontë, *Jane Eyre* (1850; New York: Cambridge University Press, 1997).

Philip K. Dick, *Do Androids Dream of Electric Sheep?* (New York: Bantam, 1982).

Amy Heckerling, *Clueless* (Paramount, 1995).

Baz Luhrmann, *Romeo and Juliet* (Columbia, 1999).

Valerie Martin, *Mary Reilly* (New York: Doubleday, 1990).

Jean Rhys, *Wide Sargasso Sea* (New York: Norton, 1996).

Ridley Scott, *Blade Runner* (Columbia, 1982).

Anne Sexton, *Transformations* (Boston: Houghton, 1971).

Robert Louis Stevenson, *The Strange Case of Dr Jekyll and Mr Hyde* (1886; New York: Dover, 1991).

Wide Sargasso Sea by imagining the first wife of Rochester as a girl torn from her home in the West Indies and transported to the cold of England. Anne Sexton retells the tales of the Brothers Grimm as glimpses into the vicissitudes of middle age in her troubling series of poems, *Transformations*. Films also often bring novels and plays to the screen, of course, sometimes in fairly earnest, faithful, and uninteresting ways, but often in a manner that sharply distinguishes the movie from book. In *Blade Runner*, for instance, Ridley Scott recasts Philip K. Dick's dystopic novella *Do Androids Dream of Electric Sheep?* as an edgy and stylish film noir thriller. Amy Heckerling's *Clueless* cleverly reimagines Jane Austen's *Emma* as a 1990s Valley Girl, and Baz Luhrmann offers Romeo and Juliet as lovers in a nightmarish and gang-ridden future. I could cite examples indefinitely, and I'm sure that you could add several of your own to my list. But that's my point: Reworking familiar materials is standard artistic practice. And much as many creative artists transform prior texts into new works of their own, so, too, academics often rewrite the approaches of thinkers who have influenced them.

Projects

Defining an Approach

Locate an academic essay or book that you admire. See if you can describe its impact on you as a reader in two ways— first through defining its *project* along the lines I suggested in chapter 1, and then through defining the *approach* of its writer as I've discussed here. Think of your task in defining her or his approach as describing what you would need to be able to do in order to work in the mode or spirit of this particular writer.

But while creative artists often reshape plots or images that strike them as somehow troubling or flawed, so that the new version of a work functions as a criticism of the older text, academic writers tend to make a more generous and sympathetic use of their influences. Another way of putting this contrast might be to say that while artists often take new approaches to familiar materials, intellectuals tend to embrace an approach in order to extend it to new questions and texts. (Perhaps it seems counterintuitive to model an intellectual project on work that strikes you as deeply misguided or flawed?) In this sense taking an approach differs from the more critical practice of countering. But it differs as well from forwarding in its attempt to draw on and make use of not just a particular phrase or idea from a text but the intellectual style or sensibility of its writer—her or his defining concerns, methods, and values. The mode of a writer is not always evident in the conclusions she reaches or the ideas she advances; it has more to do with *how* she reaches her conclusions, *how* she deals with ideas—with the kinds of problems that interest her and the characteristic ways she goes about responding to them. A mode is not so much a style of writing as a style of thinking; it is often revealed in characteristic turns of phrase but it is not reducible to them. You can't write in the mode of John Berger, for instance, simply by employing short sentences and one-line paragraphs. You also need to connect such uses of language to his broader intellectual concerns—as well as to your own. You need to forward a style not of phrasing but of approach.

Allow me to illustrate this point with an example from my own work. A few years ago I wrote a book on the history of the teaching of writing in U.S. colleges. Several other scholars had written before on this subject, but I felt uneasy with the view of the field they tended to take, which focused for the most part on leading thinkers and the schools of thought their work gave rise to—sort of a kings-and-battles story of the profession. I wanted to write a history that centered instead on the tensions and conflicts that drove work in the field, on the problems that my profession had somehow ended up addressing, rather than on the accomplishments of individual scholars and teachers. I found a model of this sort of study in a book called *Keywords* by the British cultural critic Raymond Williams. In this book Williams shows how the meanings of many of the words we use to talk about issues in culture and society—including terms like *culture* and *society* but also *art, class, democracy, popular, work,* and so on—have evolved over time. It is an odd and remarkable book. I saw in it a way of condensing a history of conflict and debate into a set of a few highly contested terms—and I ended up structuring my book around five such terms in the teaching of writing (*growth, voice, process, error,* and *community*). In that sense I felt that my book was written in the mode of Williams. (I cite Williams on *interest* in the introduction of this book, and you can probably also see some of his influence in the structure of these chapters.) But I didn't try to imitate Williams's style as a writer, which I find rather pedestrian, or to adopt his particular approach to analyzing keywords, which is more that of a philologist than an essayist. My book thus offered a *version* of what I had seen in *Keywords;* I had not so much adopted a method from Williams as taken my cue from his approach.

Whether I was successful or not is for others to say. I draw on my experience here simply to suggest what it might mean to try to work loosely but appreciatively in the mode of another. "Who are your influences?" band manager Jimmy Rabbitte asks the musicians who have answered his ad in *The Commitments*—and only those with a good answer earn an audition. ("Clarence Clemons, the Muppets, and the man from Madness," responds the saxophone player who gets the

Intertexts

Joseph Harris, *A Teaching Subject: Composition since 1966* (Englewood Cliffs, NJ: Prentice Hall, 1997).

Raymond Williams, *Keywords: A Vocabulary of Culture and Society,* rev. ed. (New York: Oxford University Press, 1983).

You will recall that I also suggested in the introduction that I see *this* book as following a lead offered by J. L. Austin in his *How to do Things with Words,* 2nd ed. (Cambridge, MA: Harvard University Press, 1962).

job.) Writers have similar sorts of influences. They are the thinkers who shape our work in deep and pervasive ways. And so defining the mode of another writer very often means describing what attracts you to her work, so readers can then lis-

Intertexts

See both Roddy Doyle's novel *The Commitments* (New York: Vintage, 1989) and Allen Parker's rousing 1991 film adaptation of it (Fox).

ten for her influences on your writing and thinking. But *working* in the mode of another involves, again, pushing beyond that influence. My aim in this chapter is thus to offer you some strategies for both acknowledging your influences and transforming them—that is, for taking on an approach and rewriting it, making it your own.

These strategies are harder to describe than the moves of coming to terms, forwarding, and countering, since they involve citing not particular phrases or ideas but an entire style or perspective, adapting not a specific text but a mode of thinking and writing. Still, I see at least three distinctive ways of positioning your own work in relation to that of writers and intellectuals who have shaped your approach:

- *Acknowledging influences:* Noting those writers whose work has in some way provided a model for your own.
- *Turning an approach on itself:* Asking the same questions of a writer that he or she asks of others.
- *Reflexivity:* Noting and reflecting on the key choices you have made (concerning method, values, language) in constructing your text.

In thus situating your own approach as a writer you can begin to rewrite not simply a specific text or idea but a broader style of thinking and working.

Acknowledging Influences

In trying to describe how a certain writer has influenced your own work, you may find it useful to consider these aspects of her or his approach:

- *Defining concerns:* What kinds of problems does this writer typically take on? What sorts of questions does she or he ask? What types of texts or materials tend to attract his or her attention?

What drives the writer's work, what interests or values seem most at stake?

- *Characteristic methods:* How does the writer go about answering the problems posed or the questions asked? Does he or she interview or observe others? Survey previous research? Look at historical contexts? Analyze the language of texts? Reflect on his own experiences?

- *Style:* What sort of person do you sense behind the writing? Are there particular qualities that you admire? A sense of wit or humor, perhaps? A generosity in dealing with the work of others? A willingness to take unpopular stands?

Remember, though, that in defining the approach of a writer, you are not trying to describe a person so much as a way of writing and thinking. You can't become someone else, but you can take on (and rewrite) someone else's way of working.

Let me turn to an example of a writer as he tries both to acknowledge someone who has had a strong impact on his thought and to describe how he has modified and rewritten that influence. The following passage comes from Richard Sennett's introduction to *Flesh and Stone,* a study of how the designed environment of cities—their buildings, streets, monuments, and open spaces—embodies the values of the people who work and dwell in them.

> I began studying the history of the body with the late Michel Foucault, a collaboration we started together in the late 1970s. My friend's influence may be felt everywhere in these pages. When I resumed this history a few years after his death, I did not continue as we had begun.
>
> In the books for which is he most well known, such as *Discipline and Punish,* Foucault imagined the human body almost choked by the knot of power in society. As his own body weakened, he sought to loosen this knot; in the third published volume of his *History of Sexuality,* and even more in the notes he made for the volumes he did not live to complete, he tried to explore bodily pleasures which are not society's prisoners. A certain paranoia about control which had marked much of his life left him as he began to die. . . .
>
> In writing *Flesh and Stone* I have wanted to honor the dignity of my friend as he died, for he accepted the body in pain. . . . And for

this reason, I have shifted from the focus with which we began: exploring the body in society through the prism of sexuality. If liberating the body from Victorian sexual constraints was a great event in modern culture, this liberation also entailed the narrowing of physical sensibility to sexual desire. In *Flesh and Stone*, though I have sought to incorporate questions of sexuality into the theme of bodily awareness of other people, I have emphasized awareness of pain as much as promises of pleasure. This theme honors a Judeo-Christian belief in the spiritual knowledge to be gained in the body, and it is as a believer that I have written this book. I have sought to show how those who have been exiled from the Garden might find a home in the city.

> ### Intertexts
>
> Richard Sennett, *Flesh and Stone: The Body and City in Western Civilization* (New York: Norton, 1994), 25–26.
>
> Sennett refers here to two books by the French social historian and philosopher Michel Foucault: *Discipline and Punish* (New York: Pantheon, 1977) and *The History of Sexuality: The Care of the Self* (New York: Vintage, 1988).

Sennett is an American sociologist whose interest in public life is mirrored by a plain style of writing addressed to both specialists and common readers. Michel Foucault was a French social theorist whose interest in the covert dynamics of power found expression in notoriously convoluted and difficult prose. And so while Sennett speaks here of the pervasive influence that Foucault had on his work, it is not a connection that many readers might have made on their own. Indeed, Sennett doesn't even cite Foucault in the rest of *Flesh and Stone*. This is not a routine thanks, then, but a way for Sennett to align his book with another set of investigations into the body in society. That is to say, in this passage he is able not only to note the influence of his friend but also to situate the aim of his own writing more precisely by showing how he both follows and departs from the path suggested by Foucault. (It is of course also unusual—and complicating—that Sennett is talking about the work of someone he considers to have been a friend, but my interest here is in the intellectual connections he draws between their projects.)

Notice how Sennett describes not only the focus of Foucault's project, "exploring the body in society through the prism of sexuality," but also its characteristic tone, his "paranoia about control" and his hope that sex could somehow liberate the body from that control. Sennett then distances himself from Foucault through offering a quiet critique of both this focus and tone, suggesting that he now finds "the narrowing of physical sensibility to sexual desire" to be confining, and so he has felt the need in writing to emphasize "awareness of pain as much as promises of pleasure." And so, finally, Sennett hints that he will look at cities not as structures of constraint and power, as Foucault might have encouraged, but rather as attempts to build a home in a fallen world.

There seems to me quite a lot going on in this short and graceful passage, perhaps more than I can really get at without offering much more elaborate accounts of the work of both Sennett and Foucault. But I hope that I have suggested through this example how acknowledging influences can serve as a way not simply of paying intellectual debts but of positioning your own project as a writer. You can glean a number of tactics for doing so from Sennett:

- *Acknowledge deep influences:* Take the time to note work that has influenced you but that you may not discuss at length later on in your text. Think of yourself as offering your readers a context for understanding your project, a sense of where you are writing from.
- *Define how those influences have directed your work:* This often has as much to do with someone's style of approach as with his central ideas. Sennett, for instance, speaks of his desire not only to continue Foucault's studies of the body in society but to do so in a way that reflects a certain "dignity" that he feels marked his friend's later work.
- *But also show how your approach diverges from theirs.* "My friend's influence may be felt everywhere in these pages . . . [but] I did not continue as we had begun." If you cannot write a sentence of this sort (whether or not it makes it way into the final version of your essay), then you are not making use of your influences, you are simply applying them.

Turning an Approach on Itself

Sennett offers an example of a writer bringing to the surface an influence on his work that might otherwise not have been apparent. But there is another and perhaps even more self-reflexive way of taking on the mode of someone else—and that is to turn an approach back on itself, to ask a writer the same sort of questions that she or he asks about others. Or, to put it another way, you can sometimes take both your subject and method of analysis from the texts you are working with.

An example will help show what I mean. In *The Metaphysical Club,* Louis Menand offers a social history of what has been called the only homegrown American school of philosophy, pragmatism, as found in the writings of Oliver Wendell Holmes, William James, C. S. Pierce, and John Dewey. Here is how Menand describes his project near the start of his book:

> If we strain out the differences, personal and philosophical, they had with one another, we can say that what these four thinkers had in common was not a group of ideas, but a single idea—an idea about ideas. They all believed that ideas are not "out there" waiting to be discovered, but are tools—like forks and knives and microchips—that people devise to cope with the world in which they find themselves. They believed that ideas are produced not by individuals but by groups of individuals—that ideas are social. They believed that ideas do not develop according to some inner logic of their own, but are entirely dependent, like germs, on their human carriers and their environment. And they believed that since ideas are provisional responses to particular and unreproducible circumstances, their survival depends not on their immutability but on their adaptability.
>
> The belief that ideas should never become ideologies—either justifying the status quo, or dictating some transcendent imperative for renouncing it—was the essence of what they taught. In many was this was a liberating attitude, and it accounts for the popularity that Holmes, James, and Dewey (Pierce is a special case) enjoyed in their lifetimes, and for the effect that they had on a whole generation of judges, teachers, journalists, philosophers, psychologists, social scientists, law professors, and even poets. They taught a kind of skepticism that helped people cope with life in a heterogeneous, industrialized,

Intertexts

Louis Menand, *The Metaphysical Club: A Story of Ideas in America* (New York: Farrar, Straus, & Giroux, 2001), xi–xii.

Cornell West, whom I quoted earlier in this book, also offers a provocative and politicized reading of the pragmatists in *The American Evasion of Philosophy* (Madison: University of Wisconsin Press, 1989).

mass-market society; a society in which older bonds of custom and community seemed to have become attenuated, and to have been replaced by more impersonal networks of obligation and authority. But skepticism is also one of the qualities that make societies like that work. It is what permits the continual state of upheaval that capitalism thrives on. . . .

This book is an effort to write about these ideas in their own spirit—that is, to try to see ideas as always soaked through by the personal and social situations in which we find them. Holmes, James, Pierce, and Dewey were philosophers, and their work is part of the history of abstract thought. Its philosophical merits were contested in its own time, and they are contested today. This book is not a work of philosophical argument, though; it is a work of historical interpretation. It describes a change in American life by looking at a change in its intellectual assumptions.

Projects

Rewriting Rewriting

Suppose you were asked to turn the approach of this book on itself. How would you define its approach? What questions would you ask of it? In what ways—or not—does this book enact the approach it talks about? In what ways does it do something else?

This passage might be used to illustrate each of the writerly moves I have discussed so far in this book. Menand begins by coming to terms with the pragmatist project through defining its central "idea about ideas"—the notion that ideas are tools used to get things done in the world. He then counters that idea, noting that while the more skeptical attitudes fostered by pragmatism helped people cope with life in mass society, they also allowed for "the continual state of upheaval that capitalism thrives on." And he then says that he will take on the approach of the pragmatists as his own, to forward their thinking in his book through trying to "see ideas as always soaked through by the personal and social situations in which we find them."

But what makes Menand's project even more interesting is his effort to apply the views of the pragmatist philosophers to an analysis of *their own work*, "to write about these ideas in their own spirit." So ideas are tools to get things done? Well, then, what does the idea that ideas are tools help us to do? So ideas need to be understood within a social context? Well, what social context gave rise to *that* idea? And so Menand turns the approach of the pragmatists back on itself, takes on their way of thinking in order to question and transform it.

I admire how Menand adopts the approach of the pragmatists but also insists on using their ideas to his own ends. He writes not as a philosopher but as a cultural historian, not as an acolyte of James and Dewey but as someone who is trying to understand the roles they played in changing American attitudes and society. He thus needs both to think like a pragmatist and to see the problems in doing so, to alternate between an appreciative use of and a skeptical view toward their work. That is the dialectic of intellectual prose.

Reflexivity

I have so far described the conscious taking of an approach as a way of situating your own project in relation to the defining methods and concerns of other writers. But there are often other sorts of influences on your writing that you need to reckon with as well. One of the characteristic features of academic writing is its *reflexivity*—those moments in a text when a writer reflects on the choices that she or he has made in taking a certain approach or in making use of a particular term. Such reflexive moves often (though not always) are made near the beginning of a text, as a kind of clearing of space for the writer's project. But not all influences on a project are easily cited or described. The values and experiences, even the very forms of language, that a writer brings to his work can sometimes profoundly shape his text. Let me close this chapter, then, with some thoughts on how you might thoughtfully acknowledge the other kinds of influences on your writing.

Academic writing is often dogged by worries about bias. How might the experiences, values, beliefs, or politics that you bring to a subject shape what you can find to say about it? One response to this problem has been to urge writers to bracket out such commitments, to strive instead for a distanced and impartial view of their subjects. Unfortunately, this goal also removes the reason most of us have for writing in the first place—which is to explore subjects that matter in some real way to us. The question, then, is not how to attain a state of Olympian disinterest but how to account in an open way for the experiences and values that drive your work as a writer.

You can see Harry Braverman struggling with this issue in the opening pages of his study of the de-skilling of work in the last century, *Labor and Monopoly Capital*. Braverman writes of how he worked for many years as a highly trained coppersmith before eventually moving on become an editor in a publishing office and, finally, a scholar and writer. Since his book is about how industrialization has over time reduced the need for a skilled workforce, gradually replacing trained artisans with unskilled laborers, he worries that some readers will suspect that the rigor of his thought has been compromised by his anger at the decline of craftsmanship. Here is how Braverman responds to this concern:

> I had the opportunity of seeing at first hand, during those years, not only the transformation of industrial processes but the manner in which those processes are reorganized; how the worker, systematically robbed of a craft heritage, is given little or nothing to take in its place. Like all craftsmen, even the most inarticulate, I always resented this, and as I reread these pages I find in them a sense not only of social outrage, which was intended, but also perhaps of personal affront....
>
> As the reader will see in the appropriate chapters, I have tried to put this experience to some

---

Intertexts

Harry Braverman, *Labor and Monopoly Capital: The Degradation of Work in the Twentieth Century* (New York: Monthly Review Press, 1974), 6–8.

---

use in this book. I have also had the benefit of many conversations—with friends, acquaintances, strangers met at social gatherings or while traveling—about their work (and it may be that some of them, if they chance to read this, will now understand why I was curious to the point of rudeness). But while this occupational and conversational background has been useful, I must emphasize that nothing in this book relies upon personal experiences or reminiscences, and that I have in the formal sense included almost no factual materials for which I could not give a reference which can be checked independently, as is proper in any scientific work.

I am awed by Braverman's sense of scruple. On the one hand, he openly admits to a sense of outrage, resentment, and affront, stemming from his experiences as a skilled worker, that motivates his study and colors his prose; on the other, he insists that his argument does not rely at any point on such insider knowledge alone. This is a subtle move, since in the very act of asserting that he will *not* authorize his study in his experiences as a coppersmith, Braverman in effect does precisely that. For certainly for readers like myself, knowing that Braverman has been trained as both a craftsman and economist lends his study of skilled labor a special authority. But there is nonetheless a strong point to be made in distinguishing between the commitments and values that bring a writer to a certain project and the methods by which he then proceeds—and Braverman proves good to his word in the rest of *Labor and Monopoly Capital,* referring assiduously to public texts rather than personal experience to ground his claims about the gradual deskilling (and thus disempowerment) of craft workers and artisans. He does not claim to be disinterested but he does strive to be rigorous and fair.

The historian Doris Kearns Goodwin offers a similar insight into the need to ground public claims in something more than personal experience and memory in *Wait Till Next Year,* a book that mixes memoir and social history. Goodwin centers her book on her recollections of her girlhood as a Brooklyn Dodger fan in the 1950s, the era of both their greatest disappointments and triumphs. But she also has a larger point to make about how neighborhood residents can use sports teams to forge a sense of community—along with a desire to make sure that what she remembers is in fact what happened. Here is what she says about her method in writing *Wait Till Next Year:*

Intertexts

Doris Kearns Goodwin, *Wait Till Next Year* (New York: Simon & Schuster, 1997), 10–11.

I soon discovered, however, that my own memory was not equal to my expanding ambition. Some of my most vivid private recollections of people and events seemed ambiguous and fragmentary when subjected to the necessities of public narrative. If I were to be faithful to my tale, it would be necessary to summon to my own history the tools I had acquired in investigating the history of others. I would look for evidence, not simply to confirm my own memory, but to stimulate it and to provide a larger context for my childhood adventures. Thus I sought out the companions of my youth, finding almost everyone who lived on my block, people I hadn't seen in three or four decades. I explored the streets and shops in which I had spent my days, searched the Rockville Centre archives, and read the local newspapers from the fifties. From all this—from my own memory and the extended memory of others, from old pamphlets, documents, yearbooks, and photo albums—I have tried to re-create the life of a young girl growing up in a very special time and circumstance, and set upon a path which led inexorably to a place she could not even imagine.

As a historian, Goodwin is used to dealing with a variety of texts: interviews, newspaper clippings, pamphlets, yearbooks, and the like. As a memoirist, she is writing in a quite different genre than most of the writers I quote in this book, one that privileges experience far more than most sorts of academic or intellectual prose. And yet I think her impulse is much the same as Braverman's—which is to make sure that her memories of what she experienced connect with what others have said about her subject. For me the key phrase in Goodwin's passage is "the necessities of public narrative"—which seems to me a version of Braverman's references "which can be checked independently." Neither writer wants to base what she or he has to say on the "ambiguous and fragmentary" evidence of experience and memory alone. But neither wants to disown or bracket out the values that drive her or his work. The need to find a way to connect evidence with values, to acknowledge inevitable bias and to check against it, is what prompts the reflexive moment for both.

As a writer you can't help but begin work on a project with a certain set of experiences, values, and commitments. This is why academics prize the sort of reflexivity shown by Braverman and Goodwin. But there is still another sort of given that you often need to acknowledge as you start to write, and that is the language. I am not being facetious. One of the problems facing a writer beginning work on a subject is what to name it. For on the one hand, the words commonly used to refer to a certain subject or idea can often seem clumsy and inexact; on the other, their previous uses can often suggest meanings that you may not desire. The use of technical terms or neologisms avoids this problem, but also creates another one, since many readers may feel distanced by a specialized vocabulary. The psychologist Bruno Bettelheim offers a vivid example of the possible consequences of such choices in his book on *Freud and Man's Soul.* Bettelheim argues that Freud intended psychoanalysis to be something more like an interpretive art than a clinical procedure, but that the translators of his work into English replaced many of Freud's deliberate uses of ordinary German words with Latinate terms in order to lend an air of scientific credibility to his project. As Bettelheim observes:

> Only the wish to perceive psychoanalysis as a medical specialty can explain why three of Freud's most important new theoretical concepts were translated not into English but into a language whose most familiar use today might be for writing prescriptions. . . . In naming two of the concepts, Freud chose words that are among the first words used by every German child. To refer to the unknown, unconscious contents of the mind, he chose the personal pronoun "it" (*es*) and used it as a noun (*das Es*). But the meaning of the term "the it" gained its full impact only after Freud used it in conjunction with the pronoun "I" (*ich*), also used as a noun (*das Ich*). His intended meanings found their clear expression in the title of his

Intertexts

Bruno Bettelheim, *Freud and Man's Soul* (New York: Knopf, 1982), 52–53.
   Freud's *The Ego and the Id* (not *The I and the It*) (1914) is reprinted in *The Standard Edition of the Complete Psychological Works,* vol. 14, ed. and trans. James Strachey (London: Hogarth, 1961).

book—*Das Ich und das Es*—in which he defined those concepts for the first time, as counterparts of each other. The translation of these personal pronouns into their Latin equivalents—the "ego" and the "id"—rather than their English ones turned them into cold technical terms, which arouse no personal associations.

I recall being startled when I first read this passage, not by the specific choices that Freud's translators had made (for which I can see justifications), but simply by discovering that in fact such choices *had been made*—and then, evidently, forgotten. As someone who had taken the usual introductory college courses in psychology and read the usual smattering of Freud, I felt familiar with the concepts of the *ego* and the *id,* but I had until that point always assumed that those Latinate terms were coined by Freud himself. The *I* and the *it* seemed altogether something else. In reading Bettelheim, I realized that hidden from my view within the realm of psychoanalysis had been competing ways of naming and thus coming to understand—and here we confront yet another problem of finding the right name—the *psyche* or *soul* or *mind* or *self.* I began to see, that is, why intellectual writers need not only to choose their terms with care but also to explain the thinking behind their choices.

I've faced much this same problem in this book as I've tried to find names for the various moves that academic writers make. For while the usual terms for such work—*thesis, summary, analysis,* and so on—struck me as misleading, I've also wanted to use words that would make some intuitive sense to my readers. And so, for instance, since much of what I wanted to say in chapter 1 is based on my observation that academics don't often "summarize" other texts in the innocuous ways suggested by that familiar term, I realized that I needed not only to come up with an alternative name for what such writers actually do, but also to explain why I felt this new name was more useful than the old. (Whether this is in fact the case with "coming to terms" is of course now your call.) This is why so much of this book is given over to what is sometimes called *metatext*—text about text, writing about writing, moments when a writer calls attention to the terms he is using or the moves he is making (as I am doing now). Indeed, I'd argue that a use of metatext characterizes academic writing. If getting the words right matters, then how you get to those words matters, too. Metatext lets you speak directly to your readers, to say to them, in effect, *Here's why I'm approaching this subject this way*. And perhaps because such metatextual moments tend to have a behind-the-scenes feel, as you confide some of the difficulties you've faced and some of the choices you've made in composing your text, they are often moments that stand out powerfully in your writing. They help your readers understand your text from your point of view.

Metatext often takes the form of brief phrases that orient your readers to the moves you are making in an essay. *My aim here is . . . Perhaps an example will help to show . . . A problem with this line of thinking is . . . I will draw on the ideas of Berger to . . .* Such phrases serve as something like road signs in a text, alerting readers to important shifts or turns in your thinking. My main concern here, though, is with those more extended and openly reflexive bits of metatext, usually near the start of a piece, in which you map out your project as a whole. Such work usually involves discussing the possible terms either for your *subject* or for your *position*. For instance, near the start of *Fear of Falling*, the book on the anxieties of the "professional middle class" that I quoted near the end of chapter 2, Barbara Ehrenreich talks about how she settled on that particular label for the people she is writing about:

> There is even a problem with what to call this class. One measure of its status as an implicit mainstream and presumably neutral vantage point is that it has no proper and familiar name. *Middle class* is hardly satisfactory, standing as it often does for almost everyone except the extremes of wealth and poverty. *New class* is favored by intellectuals, but assumes some awareness of the "old" classes—the bourgeoisie and the proletariat—and has hence remained exotic. *Intelligentsia* is occasionally used but is far too narrow and, I think, unduly flattering. *Professional-managerial class* comes closest to describing the special status of this class, and *professional middle class*—which I will employ here—is close enough. But since that term is cumbersome to read or say, I will fall back, at times, on *middle class*.

What intrigues me here is how Ehrenreich feels the need to navigate between the demands of precision and common usage. On one end of the spectrum of use, she

> **Intertexts**
>
> Barbara Ehrenreich, *Fear of Falling: The Inner Life of the Middle Class* (New York: Harper, 1989), 5–6.

finds exact but unfortunately exotic terms like *professional-managerial class;* on the other, she is left with the plain vanilla of *middle class,* a term that everyone knows but that also ambiguously stands "for almost everyone." Ehrenreich's solution to this problem is worth noting, since she ends up creating a sort of code in which, for her purposes, *middle class* will stand for *professional-managerial class.* She inflects the meaning of the common usage, transforms it (slightly) for her use.

In his *Letters to a Young Contrarian,* Christopher Hitchens shows us a writer facing similar difficulties in naming the position or perspective he is writing from. Hitchens is known for his fiercely contentious, independent, and acerbic writings on culture and politics; one of his better-known books, for instance, is an exposé of Mother Theresa of Calcutta, someone whom almost everyone else, at least until his writing, had considered an icon of saintliness. Of all the texts I've quoted so far, *Letters to a Young Contrarian* is, in many ways, the most like my own here (although I'm not sure Hitchens would be pleased by the comparison), since it is a book of advice—in this case, of advice given in response to a student who wishes to learn "how a radical or 'contrarian' life may be lived." The problem for Hitchens, though, lies with the need he feels to put scare quotes around *contrarian.* For the somewhat heroic resonances of both that term and *radical* embarrass Hitchens, who begins *Letters* by noting that "it is a strange thing, but it remains true that our language and culture contain no proper word for your aspiration." He then goes on to propose and reject a number of other possible terms—*dissident, maverick, rebel, iconoclast*—on similar grounds, before reflecting:

> I nearly hit upon the word "dissenter" just now, which might do as a definition if it were not for certain religious and sectarian connotations. The same problem arises with "freethinker." But the latter term is probably the superior one, since it makes an essential point about thinking for oneself. The essence of the independent mind lies not in *what* it thinks, but in *how* it thinks. The term "intellectual" was originally coined by those in France who believed in the guilt of Captain Alfred Dreyfus. They thought that they were defending an organic, harmonious and ordered society against nihilism, and they deployed this contemptuous word against those they regarded as the

diseased, the introspective, the disloyal and the unsound. The word hasn't completely lost this association even now, though it is less frequently used as an insult. (And, like "Tory," "impressionist" and "suffragette," all of them originated as terms of abuse or scorn, it has been annexed by some of its targets and worn with pride.) One feels the same sense of embarrassment in claiming to be an intellectual as one does in purporting to be a dissident, but the figure of Emile Zola offers encouragement, and his singular campaign for justice is one of the imperishable examples of what may be accomplished by an individual.

Intertexts

Christopher Hitchens, *Letters to a Young Contrarian* (Cambridge, MA, Basic, 2001), 1, 3–4.

This volume is part of a series that invokes and continues the spirit of Rainier Maria Rilke's famous book of advice on writing, *Letters to a Young Poet,* trans. M.D. Herber (New York: Norton, 1954). Hitchens's book on Mother Theresa is *The Missionary Position* (London, Verso, 1997).

Hitchens then goes on to discuss Zola's efforts to free the unjustly accused Dreyfus as a case study of an intellectual (or dissenter or contrarian or whatever) in action. He thus defines his position not in the abstract but through example. (And indeed, throughout *Letters* Hitchens teaches less through precept than through the example of his own cutting and brilliant prose.) Faced with a set of imperfect terms to use in describing his perspective, he chooses to rely on none (except when more or less forced to do so in his title), and instead gestures toward a range of words and figures that, together, roughly mark out his perspective. Much as Ehrenreich does with *middle class,* Hitchens uses *contrarian* as a placeholder term for a far more complex set of meanings and attitudes. And much as Sennett names his project as Foucauldian and Menand describes his as pragmatist, so Hitchens suggests that his is Zolaesque. All of them, in doing so, hint strongly at how they wish their work to be read.

A Note on Acknowledgments

I began this chapter by defining *taking an approach* as a way of framing your aims as a writer in relation to the work of others who have influenced you. I have ended by suggesting that this is one of several *reflexive* moves valued in academic writing. I want to stress that I see all of the moves I've discussed here as being of a piece. Sennett and Menand name certain intellectual influences on their projects; Braverman and Goodwin point to the role of the experiences they bring to their writing; Ehrenreich and Hitchens raise questions about the very words they have to work with. The attitude of each writer is a mix of openness and impatience. Constraints are acknowledged so they can be responded to. Influences are noted in order to be transformed. In this sense, each of the writers in this chapter models the stance of the intellectual as I have tried to describe it.

Projects

Tracking the Labor of Writing

See if you can keep a running log of all the work you do for the next major essay you write. This log should include your notes on

- Dates and time of work
- Type of activity: locating texts, Xeroxing, reading, note-taking, planning, talking, drafting, revising, workshopping, editing, printing, etc.
- Place: library, classroom, study, kitchen, computer lab, public transit, etc.
- Technologies used: pen, paper, note cards, post-its, highlighters, photocopiers, books, journals, computers, printers, internet, fax, telephone, etc.
- Number of minutes spent on each task
- Other people consulted

The point here is to chart the ways in which the work of writing extends beyond the simple act of keyboarding or otherwise producing text—and thus to become more aware of the various forms of labor that go into writing a critical essay, the many sites where that work takes place, and the numbers of people who in some way contribute to its progress.

And yet there is always a danger to such idealizations. I've argued throughout this book that the goal of academic writing is to form your own position on a subject in response to what others have said about it. The paradox is, though, that to achieve this sort of intellectual independence you almost always require the help of others—from the friends and colleagues whom you ask to read and respond to your writing, from the people who help you in editing and designing your text, and from those who provide you with the time and support you need to complete your work. The ability to offer brief, precise, and graceful thanks for such help is one of the defining marks of a strong writer. Such thanks are often found near the beginning or end of academic books. They are usually set off as a separate section marked "Acknowledgments" or included at the end of an introduction or afterword. I advise students to form the habit of writing a note of acknowledgments at the end of an essay, and in such notes not only to name the people they wish to thank but to specify what they want to thank them for. The classmates who talked through your ideas with you, the colleague who recommended a certain book, the professor whose lecture suggested a useful perspective, the librarian who helped you locate key texts, the roommate who assisted with proofreading, the tech person who showed you how to scan images into documents, the organization that provided support for your research, the friends and family who put up with you when you could think and talk about nothing else but what you were writing—all of these people merit your thanks. Writing is real labor. It requires real time and resources to research, read, draft, revise, and prepare the final copy of a text. And this material work of writing, of the making of texts, almost always involves the help of others.

In taking an approach, you rewrite not passages or ideas from a text but another writer's mode or style of working. For many intellectuals this sorting through of influences is the project not just of a book or essay but of a career, as in piece after piece we rethink our relationships toward those writers and teachers who have powerfully shaped our own thought and work. In talking here about taking an approach, then, I hope not so much to define a discrete move with texts that you might expect to quickly learn and master as to offer a sense of what most drives the work of many intellectuals and writers. For it is in thinking through your stance toward those writers who matter the most to you that you will begin to form your own voice as an intellectual. That is the creative paradox of academic work. And so, in the next and final chapter of this book, I will turn to the question of how to reread and rethink your own work-in-progress, to develop your own style through rewriting.

Projects

Tracking Influences

Get a couple of colored pens or highlighters and go back through an essay you plan to revise. Highlight any lines in your writing where you refer to, quote from, describe, or analyze another text. Then, in the margin, note the *name* of that text (e.g., "Berger" or "Dodge commercial") and the *use* you are making of it at that point in your essay. (If you have trouble doing so, then you know right off that you have more work to do.) By the time you reach the end of your essay, you will thus have created a kind of color-coded map of the texts you are working with and the moves you are making with them.

Go through your piece again, this time concentrating on those blocks of prose that you left *unmarked* before. Ask yourself: Where do these words and ideas come from? Or put another way: Where did you acquire this way of thinking and speaking? There are many possible answers: school, church, work, family, community, politics, sports, popular culture, and so on. See if you can then jot down in the margin some terms that describe the *perspective* you are taking at that point in your essay—the values and experiences that underlie the moves you are making with texts in your writing. Also mark those passages or phrasings in your prose that seem most clearly to indicate that perspective.

And then, finally, see if you can highlight those moments in your essay when you feel you have written something that cannot be easily predicted by either the texts you are dealing with or the values that drive your writing. Look for those moments, that is, where your ideas come through most clearly in your text. These are the points in your essay that the rest of your work leads up to. In revising you can now consider how to make those moments more visible and compelling.

5

Revising

First Draft of Paper Inadvertently Becomes Final Draft
*EUGENE, OR—The first draft of an English 140 paper by University
of Oregon sophomore Marty Blain ultimately became the final draft,
Blain reported Monday. "I was gonna keep working on it and add a
bunch of stuff about how the guy who wrote* [The Great Gatsby] *was
affected by a lot of the stuff going on around him," she said. "But then
I was like, fuck it." Blair said that she spent the time that would have
been devoted to revision watching* Friends *in her dorm's TV lounge.*
                                    —The Onion, September 27, 2000

I'm dying for some action
I'm sick of sitting 'round here trying to
write this book.
                    —Bruce Springsteen, "Dancing in the Dark"

S o far in this book I've offered you four moves for rewriting—for
making the words, ideas, and images of others part of your own
project as a writer. In this last chapter, I propose some ways of using
those moves in *revising*—that is, in rethinking, refining, and developing—
your own work-in-progress as writer. *Revising* is thus a particular form of
what throughout this book I've called *rewriting;* it names the work of returning to a draft of a text you've written in order to make your thinking in
it more nuanced, precise, suggestive, and interesting.

My method here will be to work in the mode of the previous four chapters—to ask what it might mean to come to terms with, forward, counter,

or take the approach of your own text-in-progress. My hope is that doing so will allow me offer a view of revising that, on the one hand, doesn't reduce it to a mere fiddling with sentences, to editing for style and correctness, but that also, on the other hand, avoids lapsing into mystical exhortations for risk taking or critical self-awareness or some other vague but evidently desirable quality of mind. My aim is instead to describe revising as a knowable practice, as a consistent set of questions you can ask of a draft of an essay that you are working on:

- *What's your project?* What do you want to accomplish in this essay? (Coming to Terms)
- *What works?* How can you build on the strengths of your draft? (Forwarding)
- *What else might be said?* How might you acknowledge other views and possibilities? (Countering)
- *What's next?* What are the implications of what you have to say? (Taking an Approach)

While these questions are straightforward, they are not easy. Revising is the sort of thing that is fairly simple to describe but very hard to do well—like playing chess, or serving in tennis, or teaching a class. It is also an activity that tends to be hidden from view. As readers we usually come upon texts in their final form—with many of the hesitations, repetitions, digressions, false starts, alternative phrasings, inconsistencies, speculations, infelicities, and flat-out mistakes of earlier drafts smoothed over, corrected, or erased. Another way to put this is to say that finished texts tend to conceal much of the labor involved in writing them. Since we rarely get to see the early drafts of most published texts, it can often seem as though other writers work, as it were, without ever blotting a line, confidently progressing through their texts from start to finish, paragraph to paragraph, chapter to chapter, as if they were speaking them aloud. This one-draft view of writing is reinforced by most movie and TV depictions of writers at work, as we watch them quickly type perfectly balanced and sequenced sentences until, with a sigh of satisfaction, they pound out THE END or press SEND. It is also a view inculcated by the pace and structure of American schooling, whose frequent exams reward students who can produce quick clean essays on demand. A result is that much of what little instruction that does get offered in writing tends to focus on questions of correctness. Handbooks are filled with advice on proofreading and teachers downgrade for mistakes in grammar and spelling.

But while the moments of both inspiration and correction, of creating a text and fixing its errors, are well marked in our culture, the work of revision, of rethinking and reshaping a text, is rarely noted. With the exception of a few literati who, in anticipation of future biographies and critical editions, seem to save all their papers, early drafts tend to get cleared off the desk or deleted from the hard drive once a project is finished, or even as it is being written. In fact, one of the few places where you can readily trace how a project evolves from one draft to the next—and thus make the labor of writing it more visible—is in a university writing course. Several of the examples in this chapter are thus drawn, with their permission, from the writings of students in courses I have taught. Each is an example of a student working with—commenting on, analyzing, rethinking—a draft of his or her own writing. For that is perhaps the key challenge of revising, to find a way to step outside of your own thinking and to look at the text you are working on as another reader might. But before looking at strategies for revising in detail, let me briefly distinguish it from two other important forms of work on an academic essay.

Drafting, Revising, Editing

For most academic writers, work on a piece begins long before they sit down at a keyboard or desk and continues well past their first attempts at putting their thoughts into prose. They tend, that is, to imagine a text they are writing less as a performance (which is what an exam calls for) and more as a work-in-progress, as an ongoing project that they can add to and reshape over time. And while the working habits of individual writers are too varied to be generalized into a single process of composing, you can think of the labor of writing as involving:

- Drafting, or generating text.
- Revising, or working with the text you've created, rethinking and reshaping what you want to say.

- Editing, or working on your text as an artifact, preparing the final version of your document.

The three form an intuitive sequence: First, you move from ideas to words on the screen or page; next you reconsider and rework what you've written, often with the help of responses from readers; and, finally, you edit, design, and format your final document. In practice, though, these forms of work tend to be overlapping and recursive: Most writers do some amount of revising and editing as they draft (although it is usually wise not to invest too much time in polishing a passage before you know for sure if you will even include it in the final version of your text); serious revision almost always involves the drafting of some new prose; and the careful editing of a piece can often lead back into a more extensive revising of it.

By far the most elusive of these three forms of work is drafting—or what is sometimes called *invention.* Trying to figure out something to write about has been the frustration of writing students—and their teachers—for decades. Stephen King puts the problem with his usual plainspoken acuity in his novel *Misery*—in which the writer of a popular series of paperback romances is held hostage by a demented fan and forced to write a new book to her liking. (In other words, the novel is about a writing class.) Here are the thoughts of King's captive author as he desperately tries to get started on his new book:

> Another part of him was furiously trying out ideas, rejecting them, trying to combine them, rejecting the combinations. He sensed this going on but had no direct contact with it and wanted none. It was dirty down there in the sweatshops.
>
> He understood what he was doing now as TRYING TO HAVE AN IDEA. TRYING TO HAVE AN IDEA wasn't the same thing as GETTING AN IDEA. GETTING AN IDEA was a more humble way of saying *I am inspired,* or *Eureka! My muse has spoken!* ...
>
> This other process—TRYING TO HAVE AN IDEA—was nowhere near as exalted or exalting, but it was every bit as mysterious and every bit as necessary. Because when you were writing a novel you almost always got

> **Intertexts**
>
> Stephen King, *Misery* (New York: Signet, 1988), 119–20.

roadblocked somewhere, and there was no sense in trying to go until you HAD AN IDEA.

His usual procedure when it was necessary to HAVE AN IDEA was to put on his coat and go for a walk. He recognized walking as good exercise, but it was boring. If you didn't have someone to talk to while you walked, a book was a necessity. But if you needed to HAVE AN IDEA, boredom could be to a roadblocked novel what chemotherapy was to a cancer patient.

I can't claim to have all that much to say about how to begin writing an essay. For me, like King, the deep origins of words and ideas seem more often than not mysterious and untraceable. But King does also offer us a number of useful ways of thinking about this mystery. First, he points to the importance of seizing hold of those ideas that do somehow come to you. The volume next to the one you were looking for on the library shelf, the comment from another class that continues to echo in your head, the connection you notice between the papers and books that happen to be sitting on your desk, the song or movie that a text reminds you of—work on an essay often begins with such serendipities. Second, King notes the value of patience, of knowing when you're stalled, when you simply need to take a break. Similarly, he speaks of the usefulness of boredom, of letting ideas percolate. Finally, he suggests that a writer often needs to start not from a moment of inspiration (*eureka!*) but from the need to work through a conceptual problem or roadblock. Indeed, I'd suggest that most academic writing begins with such questions rather than insights, with difficulties in understanding rather than moments of mastery.

What I hope I can tell you more about is how to revise a text you've begun to write, to work with the words you've started to put on the page or screen. Perhaps the most common mistake that student writers make is to slight the work of revising—either by trying to conceive and draft an entire text from start to end in a single sitting, without pausing to consider alternate (and perhaps more interesting) ways of developing their ideas, or by worrying so much about issues of editing and correctness that they hardly allow themselves to think about anything else at all. (It is only too possible, as any writing teacher can tell you, to create a text that is wonderfully designed, phrased, formatted, edited, and proofread—but that says almost nothing.) Many students enter college without really ever having been asked to rethink their views on an issue or to restructure the approach they've taken in an essay. They've been trained in how to find and fix mistakes, and perhaps even in how to respond to specific questions about a draft posed by their teacher. But their final drafts are essentially the same as their first ones—only cleaner, smoother, more polished. They have been taught how to edit but not how to revise.

In revising, the changes you make to a text are connected. They form a plan of work. For instance, if in reworking the introduction to an essay, you realize that you also need to change the order of the paragraphs that follow it, then you are revising. Or if dealing with a new example also requires you to adjust some of your key words or concepts, you are revising. Or if in re-thinking the implications of your argument at the end of an essay, you also begin to see a stronger way of beginning it, you are revising. And so on. In revising, one change leads to others. You edit sentences; you revise essays.

The changes you make in editing tend to be ad hoc and local. To edit is to fine-tune a document. Proofreading is the extreme case: You simply correct a typo or a mistake in punctuation and move on. Nothing else needs to be done; no other changes need to be made. Similarly, you can often edit for style, recast the wording of a particular sentence to make it more graceful or clear, without having to alter much (or anything) else in the paragraph of which it is part. You can even sometimes insert a sentence or two in a paragraph—to add an example, clarify a point, answer a question—while making few or no other changes to it. Indeed I've seen entire blocks of text dropped into an essay without sending any ripples at all into the paragraphs before or after it, but rather leaving the original flow of ideas serenely undisturbed. The aim of revising is to rethink the ideas and examples that drive your thinking in an essay; the aim of editing is to improve the flow and design of your document. Both forms of work are important. But simply editing a text that needs to be rethought and revised is like waxing a car that needs repairs to its engine.

Tracking Revision

You can begin to see how the work of revising differs from that of editing by mapping the changes you make in moving from one draft of an essay to the next. Most word processing programs have a "track changes" or "compare documents" tool that you can use to record the changes you make in keyboarding a new version of an essay. Using this tool allows you to mark where you

- Add to
- Delete
- Move (cut and paste)
- Rework (select and type over)
- Reformat a text you are working on.

You can of course also note and mark such changes by hand; the software simply cuts down on some of the drudgery involved.

Revising an essay is complex and difficult intellectual work. But it is work not only with ideas but text. You can't just think changes to an essay; you need to *make* them. (This is a lesson I've learned to my chagrin only too many times—as paragraphs that seemed to flow clearly in my mind when I was in the shower or out for a walk with the dogs somehow become muddled and intractable when I sit down to type them out.) At some point, that is, you have to translate plans and ideas into the material labor of adding, cutting, moving, reworking, or reformatting text. While revising clearly involves more than keyboarding, all of the work you do in rethinking a text will find its final expression in some combination of those five functions. Tracking the changes you make in keyboarding a new draft of an essay can thus help make the conceptual work you've done in revising more visible.

Let me offer an example. Here is the opening paragraph of the first draft of an essay written by Abhijit Mehta, a student in a writing course, in response to an assignment that asked him to describe some of the distinctive ways a particular group makes use of language—to reflect on how they give their own spin, as it were, to the meanings of certain words. Abhijit decided to write on the vocabulary of his own field of study, mathematics:

> The Strange Language of Math
> As our society becomes more dependant on technology, the work of mathematicians and physicists comes closer to everyday experience. In order to have a basic understanding of many modern issues and technologies, people need to become more familiar with the language

of math and science. However, mathematicians and physicists have a tendency to use common words in a strange way. In math and physics, *nice, elegant, trivial, well-behaved, charm, flavor, strange,* and *quark* all have meanings that can be very different from their everyday meanings. Mathematicians and physicists often use common words to express ideas that are very complex.

Intertexts

Abhijit Mehta, "The Playful Language of Math" (1st and 2nd drafts), unpublished essay, Duke University, 2002.

The rest of the essay follows the plan laid out in this paragraph, as Abhijit goes on to discuss the particular meanings mathematicians give to each of the terms he mentions—*nice, elegant, trivial,* and so on—in the order that he lists them. What the readers of his first draft told Abhijit, though, was that while in creating this catalogue of odd usages he had assembled the materials for an interesting essay, he hadn't yet suggested what those specialized uses told us about the culture of math. Indeed, the problem with the draft is hinted at in its title, which simply says that the language of math is "strange" but doesn't specify *how*. His readers thus asked Abhijit for a more precise sense of the attitudes and values that lay behind the usages he discussed. What *kind* of "strangeness" connected the ways mathematicians used these words?

Hard questions, but it turned out that Abhijit had answers to them. Here is the opening of his second and revised draft.

The Playful Language of Math

As our society becomes more dependent on technology, the work of mathematicians and physicists comes closer to everyday experience. In order to have a basic understanding of many modern issues and technologies, people need to become more familiar with the language of math and science. However, mathematicians and physicists have a tendency to use common words to describe complex things. In math and physics, *nice, elegant, trivial, well-behaved, charm, flavor, strange,* and *quark* all have meanings that can be very different from their everyday meanings. The migration of these words from common usage to their specialized usage conveys some of the playful attitude that mathematicians and physicists have towards abstract, complex problems.

And here is a version that maps the keyboarding changes between the two paragraphs. Words ~~deleted~~ from the first draft are struck through; text <u>added</u> to the second draft is underlined.

> The ~~Strange~~ <u>Playful</u> Language of Math
> As our society becomes more ~~dependant~~ <u>dependent</u> on technology, the work of mathematicians and physicists comes closer to everyday experience. In order to have a basic understanding of many modern issues and technologies, people need to become more familiar with the language of math and science. However, mathematicians and physicists have a ~~tendancy~~ <u>tendency</u> to use common words ~~in a strange way.~~ <u>to describe complex things.</u> In math and physics, *nice, elegant, trivial, well-behaved, charm, flavor, strange,* and *quark* all have meanings that can be very different from their everyday meanings. ~~Mathematicians and physicists often use common words to express ideas that are very complex.~~ <u>The migration of these words from common usage to their specialized usage conveys some of the playful attitude that mathematicians and physicists have towards abstract, complex problems.</u>

This map of changes shows that Abhijit was working on at least three different levels in moving from his first to second draft: At the most mundane level, he did some proofreading and corrected the spellings of *dependent* and *tendency.* Such work is simple correction, necessary but uninteresting. On a second level, he also edited for clarity and concision, combining two sentences that say almost the same thing in his first draft (mathematicians have a "tendancy to use common words in a strange way" and "often use common words to express ideas that are very complex") into a single briefer statement in the second ("a tendency to use common words to express complex things"). But while such editing helps the flow of this particular paragraph, its impact does not extend beyond it. While intelligent and helpful, it remains a local edit, unconnected to a larger pattern of revision throughout the essay.

The third level of work—what I would call *revision*—involves such a pattern and plan of change. By far the most ambitious change that Abhijit makes in his second draft is to move, in both his revised title and new last sentence, from a nebulous description of the language of math as "strange" to a more precise view of it as *playful.* These two changes signal an important shift in his project as a writer—from offering a simple catalogue of some of the strange ways that mathematicians use words to making an argument about the unexpected playfulness of the field, as evidenced by its vocabulary. In the rest of his revised essay, Abhijit goes on to identify two ways in which the playfulness of mathematicians comes into view—one in their unconventional use of common words like *nice* or *trivial* and the other in their choice of exotic and fanciful terms like *quark* to describe their concepts and discoveries. This allows him to conclude his piece by contesting the cultural stereotype of the math nerd or computer geek as a humorless drone. In short, for Abhijit the notion of play becomes a generative concept, an idea that leads to other ideas, that he uses to structure and develop the revised version of his essay.

When students in the courses I teach hand in a revised draft of an essay, I require them to include with it another copy of their text on which they track all the changes they have made in moving from one draft to the next and, more important, highlight those changes that are central to their plan of revision. I then ask them to refer to this map in writing a brief reflection on their aims and strategies in revising. (See the Projects box "Mapping Your Approach" below in this chapter for the guidelines I offer students for creating this map and reflection.) And so, for instance, a version of Abhijit's opening paragraph that boldfaced changes in **revising** (as contrasted with local proofreading or editing changes) might look something like this:

The ~~Strange~~ **Playful** Language of Math
As our society becomes more ~~dependant~~ dependent on technology, the work of mathematicians and physicists comes closer to everyday experience. In order to have a basic understanding of many modern issues and technologies, people need to become more familiar with the language of math and science. However, mathematicians and physicists have a ~~tendancy~~ tendency to use common words ~~in a strange way.~~ to describe complex things. In math and physics, *nice, elegant, trivial, well-behaved, charm, flavor, strange,* and *quark* all have meanings that can be very different from their everyday meanings. ~~Mathematicians and physicists often use common words to express ideas that are very complex.~~ **The migration of these words from common usage to their specialized usage conveys some of the playful attitude that mathematicians and physicists have towards abstract, complex problems.**

Those points throughout the rest of his revised essay where Abhijit returned to and developed the idea of the playful attitude of math would then also be boldfaced.

My aim here is not to denigrate the work of proofreading or editing. There is almost always a moment near the end of work on an essay when the most serious task that remains for you to do is to recheck and format your document with as much thought and care as you can give. (There was yet one more draft of Abhijit's essay to come, for instance, in which he noted in his opening paragraph that he would discuss *two* forms of playfulness in math, as well as made other local refinements to his prose.) Nor am I especially invested in advocating one particular method of mapping revision. What I do hope to have shown here, however, is how the local task of editing sentences and paragraphs differs in tangible and practical ways from the more global work of rethinking an essay. If in tracking the changes you've made to the draft of an essay, you can't point to a series or pattern of changes linked by an idea, then you haven't revised, you've only edited. With this sense of revising as rethinking in mind, then, let me turn to the four questions I proposed earlier.

What's Your Project? Coming to Terms With a Draft

It may seem the most banal of advice to suggest that in composing an essay you should have a good sense of your overall aim in writing, of what you want to achieve in your work, but there are at least two reasons why this truism proves harder to act upon than it might at first appear. First, while academic writers tend to begin with problems that they want to investigate, with texts that intrigue or puzzle or somehow fascinate them, their essays, when completed, need not simply to pose questions but also to respond to them. You may begin work on a project simply with the goal of finding out more about a certain subject or thinking your way through a particular set of issues, but in writing about that subject you need to articulate a stance, to establish a position of your own. The orientation of your work, that is, needs to shift as you make your way through a project. (The writing researcher and teacher Linda Flower has called this moving from *writer-based* to *reader-based* prose.) Second, you will often find that your ideas evolve over the course of writing, particularly when you are at work on an ambitious or complex project. Digressions morph into key lines of argument; examples don't quite seem to work as planned; aperçus become central ideas; afterthoughts prove more interesting than the ideas they followed; a reader's com-

Intertexts

Linda Flower, *Problem-Solving Strategies for Writing in College and the Community,* 4th ed. (New York: Heinle, 1997).

ment makes you think about your subject in unexpected ways; a small shift in phrasing leads into unforeseen avenues of thought. These are not problems to be avoided in working on an essay; they are moments to be anticipated and used.

Your project as a writer is thus something you are likely to need to rethink throughout the process of working on an essay. You may find it especially useful to revisit your purposes in writing when you have completed close to a full draft of an essay. I have often found, in rereading my work at such moments, that I seem to be looking at a different piece than the one I thought I had set out to write. The question, then, is whether to rethink what I've written in order to adhere to my original plan or to revise the plan to better describe what I've ended up writing. The answer is usually some mix of both, as my sense of my project as a whole evolves alongside my attempts to write my way through particular problems and examples.

But to test your project against your draft in such a way you need a precise and detailed account of what your aims in writing actually are. You need, that is, to come to terms with your own work. And, as I suggested in the first chapter, this involves not simply restating something like your "main idea" but rather describing your project in writing—your goals, the materials you're working on, and the moves you make with those materials. I thus often require students in my courses, once they have completed a draft of an essay, to write a brief *abstract* of their work as it then stands. (A version of this assignment appears in the Projects box "Coming to Terms with Your Own Work-in-Progress" at the end of the first chapter.) In writing such an abstract your goal should not be to reintroduce your essay but to summarize its gist for someone who has not read it. You want, that is, to write a piece that describes your essay from the outside, that distills what you have to say into as clear and pointed a form as possible.

For example, if I were to abstract the second section of this chapter—"Drafting, Revising, Editing"—I might say something like this:

> In this section I define three forms of work that go into producing an essay: *drafting, revising,* and *editing.* I suggest that while our culture both romanticizes the labor of drafting and fetishizes the importance of editing for correctness, the work of revision, of rethinking writing, often goes unnoticed and undervalued. After a brief account of the mysteries of drafting (with the help of Stephen King), I argue for distinguishing the *local* changes of editing from the *global* work of revising.

As my use of italics suggests, one aim of an abstract is to bring forward the key terms and ideas of an essay. And as the main verbs of my sentences indicate ("I define," "I suggest," and "I argue"), another goal is to identify its line of thought, the moves its writer makes. (It is up to you as my reader, of course, to decide how well I have managed to catch the gist of the previous section and what aspects of it I may have glossed over or distorted.)

The point of writing an abstract of your own work is to push you to think about the essay you are writing on two levels: (1) your project as a whole; and (2) how you develop your line of thinking. In one sense, of course, it trivializes the complexities of an essay to reduce them to a single page or paragraph, but it's also a problem if you can't offer a lucid overview of your aims in writing. If it simply seems impossible to summarize an essay that you are in the process of drafting, this may be a sign that you haven't yet quite figured out what you want to say in it. On the other hand, you also want there to be a sense of surprise and nuance in how you write out your ideas, from sentence to sentence and paragraph to paragraph, that eludes complete summary—or otherwise there will be no reason for anyone to read through your piece as whole. Forcing yourself to write an abstract of an essay you've drafted can help you move between these levels, to see where your prose advances your project effectively and where it does not. Sometimes you may find that you need to rethink how you talk about your project in order to catch up with the actual work you've done in your draft. And you are also likely to find, on a practical level, that many of the sentences you compose for your abstract end up as part of your next draft, signaling key moves or points in your argument.

Projects

Making a Revising Plan

One reason, I suspect, that many writers end up simply editing rather than revising their work-in–progress is that they approach the task haphazardly, simply trying to fix mistakes or infelicities in their texts as they happen to come across them, without ever forming a larger sense of what they want to accomplish through making such changes. To counter this tendency to fine-tune rather than rewrite, I ask students in my courses, after they've gotten feedback on a piece they are writing, to form a plan for revising their work-in-progress. We then discuss these plans before they actually begin work on the next draft of their essays. In developing their revising plans, I ask students first to write an abstract of what they have drafted so far and then:

> Offer a brief but specific plan for revision. Try as much as you can at this point to describe the substance or content of the changes you want to make. See if you can answer the following questions as precisely as you can:
>
> - Which comments from your readers—either written on your draft or offered during a workshop—have you found most useful in rethinking your essay?
> - If you plan to add to what you've written so far, what will you say and where will it go?
> - If you now plan to revise your project in writing, how will you do so? If you want to work with any different ideas or examples, what will they be?

In coming to terms with a draft, it is also often useful to counterpose the sort of overview of an essay provided by an abstract with the more narrative working through of it offered by a *sentence outline*. To create such an outline, you simply need to go through an essay, summarizing each of its paragraphs or sections in a single sentence. The result should be a kind of quick-paced version of your essay, in which it becomes clear how each of your moves and examples follows upon the other (or, sometimes, where they fail to do so). The trick in writing such a sentence outline is much like that in composing an abstract—you want to write new prose (rather than simply highlighting phrases from your text) and you want to focus less on the topics of your paragraphs than on what you are trying to do in them, on the moves you are making as a writer. And so, for instance, if I were to outline the previous section of this chapter, "Tracking Revision," I might produce something like this:

> I begin by suggesting that there are five basic types of changes that you can make in revising an essay: adding, deleting, moving, reworking, and reformatting. I then suggest that while revision can't be reduced to keyboarding, tracking keyboarding changes can make the conceptual work that goes into revising more visible. I then offer the first and second drafts of the opening paragraph of Abhijit's essay as an example of how to track changes and think about them. I start by reproducing his first draft and suggesting that there was a problem with the vagueness of "strange" as a descriptor for the language of math. Then I reproduce his second draft, first as plain text (so that readers don't get confused by all those strikeovers and underlines) and then with changes marked. Next I argue that this map of revision shows Abhijit working on three levels: proofreading, editing, and revision. I suggest that revision differs from editing in being *systematic* and *generative,* and reproduce yet one more version of Abhijit's second draft with revising changes boldfaced. Finally, I set up the next sections of the chapter by saying that I will now try to offer four strategies for rewriting (and not simply editing) your own work-in-progress.

I'll again leave it to you as my reader to decide how effective an outline of the preceding section this may be. But even though my example here is of an outline of a section in its final form, I hope you can begin to get a sense of how you could use this technique to identify moments in a text that you might want to rethink and rework. (They would be those points where you find yourself saying something like: "Well, what *am* I really trying to do here?" or "How does *this* sentence or idea follow from *that* one?") I've argued throughout this book that the strong use of the work of other writers needs to be grounded in a generous understanding of their projects. The same principle applies to your own work-in-progress. Before revising an essay, you need to articulate a clear sense of your aims in writing, so you can then assess what is working in your text and what is not.

What Works? Revising as Forwarding

An irony of revising is that writers often become so preoccupied with fixing what isn't going right in a text that they neglect to build on what is. The upshot of such attempts at remediation is often not a more interesting essay but simply one that is a little less weak. In revising you want not only to deal with the problems of a draft but also to develop its strengths. And so, when students in my courses read and respond to one another's work, I ask them to mark both those passages that strike them as especially strong and those that they have questions or worries about. (The usual code is a straight line for <u>strengths</u> and a <u>wavy</u> one for questions. You can, of course, use this system in rereading and marking your own drafts as well as in responding to the work of others.) This simple form of marking a text offers writers a map of their work that identifies those passages that their readers liked, posed questions about, or were simply indifferent toward—that no one made any particular note of. While the instinct of many writers is to let such unmarked passages stand—after all, no one has signaled them out as a problem—this third category of (non-) response more often than not points to passages that they may want to cut or abbreviate, since it is prose that has failed to draw the interest, one way or the other, of any of their readers.

You will probably want to spend most of your time reworking or developing those moments in a text that your readers have marked for either praise or question. Note that it's not always a bad sign for readers to have questions about a certain point or passage in an essay. This often means that there is something there worth thinking about, puzzling over, working through. Indeed, you can sometimes find a section of an essay both compelling and troubling at once—and I have many times seen readers mark some of the most interesting passages in an essay with both straight and wavy lines! The point is to identify those moments that have most drawn the attention of readers and to see how you can build on them, bring them forward in your next draft.

Intertexts

I learned this simple and useful code of commenting on drafts, along with many other strategies of response, from Peter Elbow's remarkable and enduring guide to running a writer's workshop, *Writing without Teachers,* 2nd ed. (New York: Oxford University Press, 2000).

Another question to ask is *where* readers mark a draft as interesting or intriguing. Often enough, you may find that several of your readers seem engaged by a sentence that appears in the middle of a paragraph in a middle page of your essay—that is, in a spot where it might well have been missed. In revising you may thus want to consider positioning that idea more prominently—perhaps at the start of the paragraph or even shifted to the opening of your essay. Or you may learn that your readers think that your most interesting work comes at the very end of your essay, on its last page or so. In such a case, you may want to see what happens if you begin your next draft with those closing ideas and see where doing so takes your thinking. This is in fact advice that I have given to many writers. The value of writing an early draft of an essay can sometimes lie in the chance it gives you to think your way through to the point, sometimes at the very end of your draft, where you've finally figured out what is you want to say. Often the best way to build on that work is not to try to salvage the fumblings of your first pages but to continue to forge ahead, to begin your next draft from the point where you ended your first.

What Else Might Be Said? Revising as Countering

Writers are often urged to anticipate the questions that readers might ask about their work, usually so that they can then preempt any possible objections to what they are trying to argue. While this advice makes some sense, it suffers from imagining the writing of an essay as the staking out of a position in a pro-con debate, and thus tends to lock a writer into defending a fixed point of view. But there is another, and I think more interesting, way of countering your own work-in-progress, and that is not simply to ask what possible objections might be raised to your work but also what *alternative* lines of thought you might want to pursue. You want to read a draft of an essay in ways that open up the possibilities of what you might say rather than lock you into a particular perspective. In revising you thus need to learn how to look at your work-in-progress not simply as a finished (or nearly finished) artifact but also as a source of ideas, a starting point for more writing.

Sometimes revising involves reworking existing text, but many other times it consists of following through on an idea or an aside, building on a suggestive turn of phrase, or taking your essay in an unplanned direction. In writing there are often moments when the best thing to do is to start over— except that you won't really be starting over, but rather beginning with an idea that's grabbed you in the midst of your work on an essay, or with a new sense of where you want to go in your thinking, or even with just a few key terms or examples that you've gleaned from the experience of working on your first draft. For instance, here is how Charles Jordan described how he rethought and redrafted an essay he was writing on Thomas Bell's novel *Out of This Furnace* for an undergraduate course in critical reading:

> My paper didn't simply evolve from a mediocre paper to an acceptable one (as I suspect most of my classmates' papers did). Rather, instead of just improving on the same paper, I wrote one with a completely different point. I started out focusing on the cyclic nature of the workers' lives and their experiences, and how the cycle was a perpetual one in which those who were in this class were trapped. However, going from first to second draft, I was asked to find something I could say at the end (or at least the middle) of my analysis that I couldn't say at the beginning. I said that I thought that my analysis validated the statement that the experiences and struggles of those in this working class actually came to define the class of people in this novel. I included something to that effect briefly in my conclusion, and in a few other places throughout the paper. However, I began to realize (not only on my own but also through the help of readers) that my initial argument of the "endless cycle" was weak, and evidence was scarce and hard to find. . . . What started out being an insightful one or two line statement in my paper started seeming more and more like an interesting argument I could make, which would also be stronger (due to more evidence). So, my paper metamorphosed from a paper trying to prove the existence of this cycle into a paper trying to show that Bell tries to define this class of workers by their struggles and sacrifices. So the major change in my paper was that my arguments and examples were

Intertexts

Charles Jordan, "Reflection on Writing," unpublished essay, Duke University, 2001.
    The essay that Charles describes in this reflection was on Thomas Bell, *Out of This Furnace* (Pittsburgh: University of Pittsburgh Press, 1976).

then framed to support this new thesis. Also, I reworded a lot of awkward phrases, and added a few more examples. . . . Besides the fact that the main argument in the paper was changed, all the other changes I made were minor, and mostly technical.

What Charles has to say here reminds me of the passage I quoted earlier by Stephen King. Both contrast the "minor and technical" work of piecing a text together with the more central problem of finding and developing its key ideas—although Charles usefully shows how such ideas can emerge not only through happenstance (as King suggests) but also through a process of talk and revision. But there is a kind of boldness, a willingness to set aside what isn't working and to build on what is, that underlies the views of both writers. Rather than simply trying to pull together evidence for a line of thought that he had begun to realize was mediocre, Charles chose the riskier path of developing another idea. I admire that. The aim of revising should not be simply to fix up or refine a text but to develop and extend what it has to say—to make your writing more precise, nuanced, inventive, and surprising. The best form of countering a work-in-progress allows for new lines of thought to emerge.

What's Next? Revising as Looking Ahead

One of the most difficult problems in writing involves figuring out how to close an essay or chapter or book before you've simply begun to repeat yourself. There's a familiar kind of academic essay that says almost everything it has to say in its first few pages—that begins, as it were, with its conclusions, laying out its thesis so mordantly in its opening paragraphs that its writer is left with little to do in the rest of the piece but to offer a set of supporting examples for points he or she has already made. The principal aim of such writing sometimes seems to be to ensure that there will be no surprises beyond the first page or two, that everything will follow the initial plan and argument as set out by the writer. The conclusions of such essays thus tend to be almost wholly ornamental, bookends whose task is simply to restate what has come before.

I have no quarrel with the need to define a clear plan of work for an essay or book. You want readers to know what your project is, to have a sense of where you're headed in your thinking and what you see as at stake in your writing. (See the Project box "Mapping Your Approach".) But you also want to *develop* a line of thinking in an essay, to explore its contradictions and stuck points and ambiguities, not simply to stake out a fixed position and defend it. You want to be able to say something at the end of an essay that you couldn't say at its start, that your work in the previous pages has made possible.

A good question to ask of a draft of an essay that you are writing, then, is at what point do you simply start to restate what you've said before? For that is where you will want to bring the piece to a close. And if your experience is like mine, you may often find in rereading a draft that you have written several pages past the point where you might have ended it. I have many times found myself wondering how to conclude a piece, only to find that I already had—although without yet realizing it. You want to finish a piece not with a ceremonial flourish, a restatement of what has come before, but with a look ahead, a gesture toward work to come, a new question or idea or insight to be followed.

Projects

Mapping Your Approach

You may find the metaphor of a *map* useful in clarifying the approach you want to take in a piece of writing. Think of this map as having two parts: an overview and road signs. The former is a passage near the start of your piece that states where you are headed in your thinking and how you will get there. For example, *In this essay I argue that . . . First, I look at . . . Then I call on . . .* An overview is often a revised version of the sort of abstract I talked about before. Road signs are brief markers throughout your text that indicate the moves you are making as a writer. In a longer piece, road signs may be section headings (as in the chapters of this book). In a shorter essay, they may be signaled by metatextual phrases like *An example of this problem is . . .* or *Some implications of this stance are . . .* or *By way of concluding, let me . . .*

First, read through your text and highlight its overview and road signs. Then, check to see if your overview really describes your essay as it now stands. Sometimes you end up in different place at the end of a piece than you thought you were headed toward at its start. Sometimes you find alternate lines of inquiry. Sometimes you simply wander off track. If your overview and essay don't correspond with each other, decide which you want to change.

Finally, check to see if you have clearly marked the turns of thought throughout your text. If you list your subheads and/or metatextual phrases, these should offer a workable outline of your essay. If not, then you may need to mark the steps of your thinking more clearly.

A powerful close to an essay or book responds to two questions: *So what?* and *What's next?* By this I don't mean that such questions are posed explicitly—they rarely are—but that readers should finish a text with a strong sense of how they have been asked to change what they feel or believe, as well as of what would be involved in continuing to think along the lines you have proposed, of what it would mean for them to take on *your* approach. In revising, then, you want to ask yourself the same question as you consider how to close an essay: How might this piece point toward new work, new writing?

It is an ambitious question—and one that you need to work toward answering throughout the whole of your essay and not simply at its conclusion. But it is not an impossible question to ask or answer. For instance, in an early draft of an analysis of the term *sketchy,* an adjective then in common use at both Duke and many other college campuses, Justin Lee concluded with this paragraph:

Sketchy has become more than a word used in context at Duke to refer to unsure ideas. It has become a transformer itself—reshaping people's attitudes and thoughts. As a sort of personal character modifier, *sketchy* is now a powerful integrity-altering word that forms a powerful impact.

While this is not a terrible close to an essay, it failed to get at the idea driving the work that Justin had done throughout his piece—which was that there was something suspect about a term, *sketchy*, that could be used to indicate vague disapproval of almost anything, without ever really indicating what the grounds for that disapproval were. And what could a reader do with the vague idea that sketchy somehow had a "powerful impact" on the "integrity" of its users? What did his analysis point toward? It was hard to say. So this is how Justin revised his closing paragraph:

> *Sketchy* has become more than a word used in context at Duke to refer to unsure ideas. It has become a transformer itself—reshaping people's attitudes and thoughts. As a sort of personal character modifier, *sketchy* is an influential character-altering word that carries a powerful impact. What I have come to discover through the course of this paper is that sketchy is also at times a less than ideal word to use. Ironically, its strength is also its weakness. To see this connection clearly, think about what makes *sketchy* a perfect word sometimes—its vagueness does. *Sketchy* carries an almost deliberate non-committal interpretation, in that it has such a wide range of uses. This means that people can say it without actually "totally taking a side," so to speak, allowing someone to voice an opinion, but also not requiring that person to "lay all of his cards down." It permits a person to half commit to a conviction without totally coming out. . . . People never really know how strongly a person is using it in context; therefore, people never know what to make of it. For this reason, the word sketchy is itself "sketchy," according to the definition and application it has taken on at Duke University—and should be used with caution.

In this new closing Justin not only offers a pointed criticism of the use of *sketchy* as a way of "half committing" yourself to an opinion but also suggests a self-reflexive

Intertexts:

Justin Lee, "*Sketchy:* A Transformer of Personal Character," unpublished essay (2nd and 3rd drafts), Duke University, 2002.

mode of analysis in which you apply the values of a term to itself. Is *sketchy* itself sketchy? How cool is cool? Is it shady to call someone else shady? Justin is thus doing new work until the very end of his piece, rather than simply concluding by restating what he has already said (as was the case in his first closing passage). And in doing so, he invites his readers to continue the work he has begun, to take up his approach, to write in his spirit.

You can imagine the work of revision, then, at its most ambitious, as pushing beyond the space of a single essay, as advancing a project whose ideas, aims, and possibilities spill over the bounds of a single piece and point toward further writing. That is what the first four chapters of this book are about: extending and rewriting the work of others. But you can also rewrite your own work in this interesting and difficult sense—to use one essay to fuel the next, to conclude not by wrapping things up but by pointing toward new lines of inquiry, by setting new tasks for yourself as a writer. Here's how another Duke undergraduate, Emily Murphy, put it in reflecting on her work on an essay in which she tried to connect the idea of "cultural capital," as formulated by a number of social theorists, to her own experiences in trying to reach out to people from other social classes. (These experiences included spending a number of days without money or shelter in order to gain some insight into the lives of homeless persons.)

> For some reason, I have a feeling that this is not the final draft of this paper—I imagine that I will revisit it again throughout my life. Therefore, although it is completely "revised" for now, it is doubtful that that is the final version. When the assignment was first given, I brainstormed lots of semi-related ideas, but I wasn't sure how I could connect them reasonably. I honestly did not think that I would use my homeless story in my piece, but when I told the story to my group, they became fascinated by it. I decided to write about being homeless and somehow relate it to our educational system, comparing myself with Cary and Kovacic. However, when I wrote the paper, I started discussing "cultural capital"—a term which I had previously just thrown around. I have learned about this term in several classes, but I have never truly considered the "cultural capital" of my high school. Once I started brainstorming, it was difficult to stop. I realized that I need to be specific, citing many examples. At this point, I knew that my paper could logically discuss my homeless experience in terms of "cultural capital." The paper began

to take shape. When I presented it, I realized that I needed to re-word some sentences because of my tone. I didn't want to appear that I was over-generalizing—after all, I am really just trying to discuss my own situation. Even though I tried to make this clear,

Intertexts

Emily Murphy, "Reflection on 'Class and Cultural Capital,'" unpublished essay, Duke University, 2001.

I still feel that the paper could be easily criticized for its overgeneralization. Throughout this week, I have continued to think of more examples or semi-related topics. It was difficult for me to actually turn in the final draft because I kept on wanting to add more. Finally, my roommate looked at me and said: "You're obsessing Em, turn it in." At this point, I do like this draft. However, I also know that I will probably write a slightly different draft after my experiences student teaching this summer. This paper will follow me, hopefully expanding and altering through time—it will be interesting to compare drafts. My room-mate knows me well—I do obsess.

Emily eloquently describes her essay here as "following" her, its shape and ideas shifting as she herself changes as a person and writer. But you might just as readily describe your project as a writer as something that is always a few steps ahead of you—that is, as something you are always reaching *toward*, only to find, at the very point you think you have at last come to the end of work on an essay or book, that there is still more writing to be done.

I've tried throughout this book to describe rewriting as an active and gener-ous use of the work of others, an attempt to keep the conversation going, *to add to* what other writers and intellectuals have thought and said about a subject. My aim here in this chapter has been to suggest how in revising you might look similarly at your own work-in-progress—that is, to view a draft of an essay not as something to be patched or fixed but as a starting point for new work, for further talk and writing. I've tried, that is, to offer a view of academic writing as a *social* practice, as a form of intellectual work that is always rooted in a set of ongoing conversations, and that is always looking to push such talk another step forward. Even so, I'm aware that I've said fairly little so far about the actual social context in which much of this work takes place—that is, about the college or university writing course. In the afterword, then, I share some of my ideas about designing and teaching courses in academic writing. But while I address this section to my fellow teachers, I hope that my brief sketch of the pace and rhythm, the feel and tone, of the sort of courses I try to teach will be of interest to students as well.

Projects

Reflecting on Revision

When students in a course I am teaching are ready to turn in the final version of an essay, I also ask them to reflect on the work they have done over the last several weeks in drafting, revising, and editing their projects. Here is what I ask them to give me:

> Along with the revised and final version of your essay, I'd like you to turn in a set of materials that trace the progress of your work in writing it. These materials will take some time and care to get ready. Please submit a folder with the following materials:
>
> - The archival version of your essay.
> - A version of your essay on which you highlight the changes you have made in moving from your first to second draft—marking those points where you have added to, cut, shifted, reworked, or reformatted your text. You can use the "compare documents" function in Microsoft Word to do much of this work, but you are likely to find that you also need to use colored pens to mark or clarify certain kinds of changes. Include a key to reading your highlights (e.g., green for added text, blue for cuts, etc.)
> - In addition to tracking these changes, you should also identify a series of connected moves that you have made in rethinking your essay—that is, to

point to a *pattern* of revision that runs through your piece. Mark this pattern clearly. You should be able to point to at least three or four linked changes at various points in your essay and to name the idea that connects them.

- A copy of the previous drafts of your essay, along with the comments of your readers on those drafts.
- Any revising plans you have created during your work on your essay.
- A brief but specific reflection on how your project has developed over the last few weeks. Drawing on the map of changes you've made, and especially the series of moves in revision you've identified, talk about the aims and strategies that have directed your work in drafting and revising your essay. How did your project in writing evolve over time? How did you come up with and carry through on your plan for revising? What went according to plan and what surprised you? If you have the opportunity to return to this piece, what further work might you want to do on it?

Afterword

Teaching Rewriting

We will teach our twisted speech
To the young believers
We will train our blue-eyed men
To be young believers.

> —Joe Strummer and Mick Jones, "Clampdown"

But I'll teach my eyes to see
Beyond these walls in front of me
And someday I'll walk out of here again.

> —Jimmy Cliff, "Trapped"

I began this book by arguing that academic writing is characterized by a responsiveness to the work of others and went on from there to offer students a set of moves for making strong and generous use of the texts they read in their own work as writers. What I have not tried to do in this book, though, is to sketch a plan for a specific sort of writing course. I have instead imagined this as a book that might be read *alongside* a wide range of other texts, that might inform a particular aspect of the work of a writing course without dictating its overall shape or focus. Indeed, I hope that this book might find use in courses in critical reading or criticism as well as composition, and at more advanced as well as introductory levels. Nonetheless, I suspect there are some things that have to go on in any course that aims to teach the practice of rewriting, of making active use of the work of others. Specifically, I think you need to:

- Ask students to write in response to complex texts and issues.
- Bring student texts regularly to the table.
- Sponsor revision by offering students the time and support they need to rethink their work-in-progress.

Let me conclude here, then, with some brief thoughts on what it means to teach a course that does such work.

Ask Students to Write in Response to Complex Texts and Issues

A good writing course teaches both a practice and a habit of mind—a way of doing things and a way of thinking about things. The work of critical response hinges on the belief that there usually is something to be said for most perspectives on an issue—and also that there is usually something that each perspective misses. It relies, that is, on a habit of mind that resists quick closure and acknowledges the merits of competing interests and values. Needless to say, this is not a mode of discourse favored by the politicians, journalists, and radio talk show hosts who are the celebrities of our current culture of partisan invective. One of the things a course in academic writing needs to do, then, is to model a different attitude toward argument, to offer students a sense of what it means to participate not in a win-lose debate but in a dialogue whose aim is to open up various possible lines of thinking.

The trick in doing so is to compose writing projects that push students beyond a simple taking of positions, that encourage the unexpected response, the third view. Indeed *three* seems to me a kind of magical number in teaching writing, since as soon as a text or assignment elicits at least three differing yet strong responses, a class can move beyond the realm of either/or debate. The question to set for a writing class is usually not *Is the author of this text right or wrong?* or even What *are the strengths and weaknesses of this position?* Such approaches tend soon to devolve into a routine and agonistic staking of claims for or against the particular text or issue at hand. Instead, the questions asked need to be something more like: *What uses can you make of this work? What else might be said on this subject?* The movement of a writing course, that is, needs to be *outward*, not losing sight

Intertexts

You will have noted that I have drawn from many of these texts for examples in previous chapters.

Roland Barthes, *Mythologies,* trans. Annette Lavers (New York: Hill & Wang, 1972).

John Seely Brown and Paul Duguid, *The Social Life of Information* (Boston: Harvard Business School Press, 2000).

Italo Calvino, *Invisible Cities* (New York: Harcourt, 1974).

Barbara Ehrenreich, *Fear of Falling: The Inner Life of the Middle Class* (New York: Harper, 1989).

George Lakoff, *Moral Politics,* 2nd ed. (Chicago: University of Chicago Press, 2002).

Plato, *Phaedrus,* trans. Alexander Nehamas and Paul Woodruff (Indianapolis: Hackett, 1995).

Anne Sexton, *Transformations* (Boston: Houghton, 1971).

I. F. Stone, *The Trial of Socrates* (Boston: Little, Brown, 1988).

Cornel West, *Race Matters* (Boston: Beacon, 1993).

Raymond Williams, *Keywords: A Vocabulary of Culture and Society,* rev. ed. (New York: Oxford University Press, 1983).

of the texts that begin an investigation but not simply fixed on them, either. The focus of work in a writing course needs to travel with the uses students make of the texts they read.

In designing a writing course, then, I look for texts open to multiple readings and uses. Doing so has for the most part led me away from the sorts of brief, pointed, and accessible essays that form the staple of many writing anthologies and instead toward longer and more ambitious texts—toward books and essays whose lines of thinking are complex and nuanced, whose form is distinctive, and whose projects are not easily summarized. I look, that is, for texts whose aims intrigue me but whose exact meanings I am not entirely sure of, and whose uses I cannot predict with certainty. The project I then usually set for students is to find a way of taking the approach of the authors we are reading. And so, for instance, I've asked students to make use of

I. F. Stone's inquest into the trial of Socrates in writing on the place of civil liberties in our current culture, to use Cornel West's thoughts on race and Barbara Ehrenreich's ideas about the professional middle class to reflect on their own social and ethnic positionings, to follow the lead of Raymond Williams in tracking the history of the uses of a key word or concept, to draw on the ideas of John Seely Brown and Paul Duguid in analyzing the social impact of a technology, to read Plato's *Phaedrus* as offering insights into how academic writing might now be taught, to expose a "myth" of popular culture in the manner of Roland Barthes, or to use the metaphors of family and society analyzed by the linguist George Lakoff in reading the discourses of an election year. And I've asked students to make a similar use of literary works as well—for instance, to use Italo Calvino's *Invisible Cities* as model for a piece of writing that is neither an argument nor a story, yet still coheres meaningfully, or to read Anne Sexton's retellings of the Brothers Grimm as a kind of how-to manual on putting a new spin on familiar materials.

In all of these cases, students must translate the approach of a writer into a working method of their own. They can't just describe Barthes, for instance; they have to *do* Barthes. This is complex and challenging work, and we take our time doing it—reading through a text closely over a number of weeks, coming to terms gradually with its project, finding and looking at some of the texts that the writer forwards or counters, slowly forming a clearer sense both of his or her approach and of the various ways each of the writers in the class might build on, extend, develop, or revise it. Rarely in the span of a semester do I have time to do such work with more than one or two books, and so I want my reading choices to count, to offer students a rich sense of what it is like to live with a text for a while, to learn its nuances and inconsistencies, and to make a full and considered use of what it has to offer.

Bring Student Writing to the Table

But a writing course is defined less through the texts you assign students to read than through the work you do with the texts that students write. I expect there to be student texts on the table at almost every meeting of a writing class that I teach. Drafts, revisions, notes, plans, proposals, exercises, responses to readings, comments on other students' essays—these are the materials of our day-to-day work together. Sometimes we look at student texts that I have selected and copied; sometimes our focus is on texts that students themselves have brought forward. Sometimes we look together at a piece of writing for the first time; often we discuss a student essay that we have all read and commented on before coming to class. Always there are copies for each of us; in a writing class, a text is something to work on, mark up, annotate. And in this sprawl of printouts and Xeroxes there also lie copies of the books we are writing about, and much of our work in class features a noisy shuffling from paper to book to paper—as we check, for instance, on the context of a passage a student writer has quoted from Plato or Ehrenreich, or look to find a section from Stone that speaks to an issue raised in another paper.

The point is for student texts to be as visible in a writing course as the texts of established authors, and thus for students to begin to see themselves as intellectuals and writers much like those authors. The teacher should not be the only person who reads the work of students; the anthology or handbook or rhetoric should not be the only text on the table in a course that claims to teach students how to write. Too often in years past students slipped their essays to the bottom of the pile as it made its slow progress toward the graybeard at the head of the table; too often now they press SEND and their work is transmitted to the electronic mailbox of their instructor. In neither case does their writing enter the public space of the classroom— and that is precisely what needs to happen. Whether read aloud, projected onscreen, photocopied, laser printed, or handwritten, student texts need to be the focus of work in a writing class. Students need to know how their classmates are approaching the same tasks they are tackling, to learn from their successes and problems, and to draw on and respond to their ideas and approaches. I always look for students who quote not only the assigned readings but also the essays that their classmates have written, or who acknowledge and thank the readers of their first drafts—for they are the ones who are imagining themselves as doing something more than schoolwork.

When I tell colleagues that student texts are brought to the table during almost every meeting of a writing class I teach, they sometimes ask me how I then also manage to teach the various books that I assign to be read. My response is that I approach these readings *through* the writings students do about them. I rarely talk about a book or essay in class before asking students to write about it. Instead, I ask them to turn in brief responses to the reading *before* we meet to discuss it in class. When we meet to talk about the text, then, we also have twelve or fifteen or twenty brief responses to it at hand. (In a digital age, you may now also be able to expect students to have read one another's responses online before coming to class.) When I turn in class, then, to *Invisible Cities* or *Moral Politics* or *The Social Life of Information,* my way into the discussion is almost always to suggest, "Well, let's begin by listening to what Sabria (or Grace or Peter or Ankur) has written about what we've read." We approach the text through their work, their writings. I thus teach not *Moral Politics* (or whatever) so much as how you go about making sense of *Moral Politics*—and then, how you put its ideas and phrasings to use in your own writing. Of course, students often fumble in their first attempts to write about a text—and many complain that they have a much better sense of what they want to say *after* we've discussed a text than they did when they tried to write about it before class. But that's the point: Strong readings of a text emerge through discussion and in response to each other. My strategy as a teacher is to ask students to commit themselves to a reading of a text, to bring that reading to the table for discussion, and then to revise the uses they want to make of the text on the basis of the work we do together.

Sponsor Revision

In this book I've set out a vocabulary for talking about some of the distinctive aims and moves of academic writing. But students in a writing course don't need to learn a vocabulary; they need to master a practice. I don't really much care if students can define *forwarding* or *countering* or any of the other terms in this book, but I do want them to be able to make the writerly moves that those terms describe. My goal as a teacher is to change what students do—how they work with other texts, and how they rethink their own prose. The moment of crisis in my teaching, then, is almost always that of the response—of how to say something useful to students about their work-in-progress.

I have often experienced this moment as one of having both too much and too little to say. There can sometimes seem a nearly unending series of comments that one might make about a piece of writing—points to add, phrasings to tinker with, readings to suggest, assertions to qualify, claims to problematize, solecisms and typos to correct—the overriding question, though, is whether any of these comments really get at the work that the writer most needs to do, or whether they are in actuality what they only too often appear to be: a list of hopeful suggestions, tentative possibilities, bursts of annoyance, and simple shots in the dark. Indeed, my impulse to write this book sprang in part from the frustration of searching for some useful way to offer what was often the only meaningful advice I felt I really had for a student writer—which was that in his next draft he should try to find something interesting to say. In many ways this book has been an attempt to explain what I mean at such moments by *interesting*.

One of the difficulties of teaching writing is that it is such a diffuse practice. The issues involved in writing a clear sentence or paragraph are not at all the same as those involved in articulating a thoughtful response to another text or in sustaining a complex line of thought over the space of several pages (or even chapters). Working writers need somehow to attend to an extraordinary and disparate set of concerns ranging from matters of stance and argument to questions of tone, phrasing, style, clarity, correctness, coherence, format, and the like. Few of us can do all of this well all of the time. In designing a writing course, then, you have to decide which aspects or moves of this almost unmanageable practice that you want to teach, and then, in responding to the work of students, you need to focus on how they make those moves.

I believe that in a course on academic writing the key questions have to do with how students make use of the work of others. In responding to drafts, then, my first concern lies always with the stances that students take toward the central texts and issues of the class. Is a student's own project as a writer clear? Does that project respond to the texts at hand? Does it in some way rewrite their ideas and phrasings? I teach students to ask these same questions when they respond to each other's writing (see the Projects box at the end of this afterword), and I reinforce this focus once more in my system of grading: To earn a C students must clearly restate the project of a text; for a B they must note moments in it of particular interest or difficulty; and for an A they must articulate a position of their own that responds to and makes strong use of its ideas and phrasings. And so, while I am happy to talk about many of the various aspects of the craft of writing as these emerge throughout the semester, I am not trying to teach students how to become "good writers" in some general sense; my goal is, rather, to help them learn how to do a specific sort of intellectual work.

That work is by its nature social and responsive. For while our cultural images of the writer at work remain centered on the author seated alone at her desk, squinting at a computer screen or scribbling on a page, in fact much of the routine and day-to-day labor involved in writing an academic essay is done with the help and in the company of others. As members of an academic seminar, students will almost surely find themselves writing in response to the texts and ideas of others, talking through ideas and questions with classmates, asking the help of librarians in finding sources, reading and commenting on the drafts of classmates, seeking the direction of teachers in revising, and drawing on the patience and skills of roommates, friends, writing center tutors, and even computer experts in editing, proofreading, formatting, designing, printing, and perhaps posting their final documents. A course in academic writing needs to guide students through this social labor. And so, once I have decided upon the issue or question that a course will investigate, I begin the task of designing the actual work of a semester by considering what kinds of writing projects I want students to take on— about the time they will need to do background reading and research, to draft their essays, to share and respond to those drafts, to revise their work, and to edit and prepare the archival versions of their writings. I also think about how much time I will need myself to respond to the various drafts, comments, proposals, and notes that will come my way; about the number of classes I will need to set aside for workshops and conferences; and about the number of classes I may want to set aside for students to present their finished work to the class. The armature of the course, that is, consists of the work to be done by students. Only once that structure is in place do I then begin to consider the readings students will need to do to inform and support their work as writers.

Let me offer a more specific example. A few years ago I offered a course on the theme of "Writing and Social Class." (I quote from some of work done by students in this class in chapter 5.) I knew that I wanted students in this course to take on two main projects as writers—one in which they looked at how the often invisible category of social class was represented in the work of a creative writer or critic, and another in which they reflected on how their own class positionings had shaped their upbringing and values. I also knew that I wanted students to present their best work to the class at the end of the semester—as a way of making the labor of revising and editing a text for publication seem real. And I knew that I wanted students to experiment with using writing not only as way of developing a position in a formal and sustained essay but also as a means of *thinking through* their responses to a set of complex texts and issues. Given those teaching goals, I was able to work *backward,* as it were, to a design for the semester: Having set aside the last two weeks for presentations, I could then allow six weeks for each of the two main writing projects. In turn, for each of those six-week projects, I was able to assign three drafts, one due every other week, and to reserve a series of class meetings to workshop those drafts. Only when I had thus determined the pace of the course—of drafts, workshops, revisions, and presentations— did I turn to the question of what texts students might read. I began my planning, that is, not with a set of assigned texts for which I then needed to create writing assignments, but with a sense of the work I wanted students to do as writers—which then led me to the readings that I hoped would help them do that work. That is the key point: A course in writing needs to be centered not on a reading list or an anthology but on a series of writing projects.

I believe that as writing teachers we need to offer students two things: The first is a sense of the moves we ourselves make as writers, of the ways we deal with texts and ideas; the second is the chance to put those moves to work for purposes of their own. In planning the work of a semester, then, I want to give students a series of chances to surprise me, to rewrite the course I have designed—to notice unexpected things about the texts I assign and to bring new texts to the table for us to talk about, to put their own spins on the familiar moves of intellectual writing, to develop their own projects as writers, to say something that responds to the work of others but that also feels new and their own. My aim, that is, is to make the writing classroom, like writing itself, a space of possibility.

Projects

Responding Toward Revision

To revise a text well you need the help of critical yet sympathetic readers who can tell you both what really works in your draft and also what you need to work more on. In any course that I teach, then, I ask students to read and talk about their work-in-progress with one another—an activity writing teachers often call *workshopping*. Here is how I ask students to prepare for such a workshop:

> In responding to an early draft of an essay, your aim should be to offer its author help in thinking about the shape and direction of her or his project as a whole. You will want, that is, not so much to offer advice about local matters of phrasing or editing but to give the author feedback about more global issues of aim, argument, example, structure, and so on. What is the author trying to get done in this essay? What does she or he do well? What kind of work does she or he need to do to make this a more interesting or compelling piece? What needs to be added? cut? reworked? rethought entirely? Your goal in responding is to help the author develop and refine his or her project before bringing it to the more public forum of our seminar.
>
> In practical terms, your response should be in two parts: Begin by writing with a brief note to the author in which you
>
> - State in a sentence or two what you see as the author's project.
> - Comment on how the author adds to the ongoing conversation of this seminar—that is, what he or she has to say about the texts and issues we've been talking about.
> - Note what works especially well in the draft—that is, any passages or ideas that seem particularly interesting, provoking, well argued, nicely illustrated, or the like.
> - Suggest one or two ways in which the author might develop, extend, qualify, or rethink the project of her or his essay. (This is *not* a moment to offer advice on editing, proofreading, or other more local matters of style and correctness.)

- Place this note at the head of the text. Address the author by name and sign yours.
- Next, having written this note, go back through the essay in order to locate three or four specific points (no more) where you think the author might do the sort of work in revision that you have suggested. Write a brief marginal comment at each of these points in the text. Make sure to connect these local comments to your opening note.

Acknowledgments

This is a short book that took a long time to write. A result has been that an unusually wide range of individuals have contributed to the writing of a slim volume—all to my gain, and I hope also to that of my readers. Several years ago, Carol Hollar-Zwick and Tony English helped me start to think about this project, and I have since watched with pleasure and admiration as Michael Spooner, the director of the Utah State University Press, has turned the manuscript I gave him into a finished book. I also owe special thanks to Robin DuBlanc for her attentive copy-editing of my text, and to Barbara Yale-Read for a cover design that enacts the elegance my prose aspires to.

When I first conceived this project, I was teaching in the English Department at the University of Pittsburgh. My approach to writing and teaching has been shaped in strong part by the years I worked in Pittsburgh, and I will always be grateful to my colleagues there—especially Dave Bartholomae, Steve Carr, and Phil Smith. I drafted and revised this book, though, while working as part of a multidisciplinary faculty in the Duke University Writing Program, and the influence of my colleagues in the UWP is everywhere to be found in these pages. My thanks go especially to Parag Budecha, Denise Comer, Van Hillard, Tim Hodgdon, David Kellogg, Jason Mahn, Derek Malone-France, Tamera Marko, Jules Odendahl-James, Marcia Rego, Michele Strano, Jim Thrall, Phil Troutman, Betsy Verhoeven, and Rebecca Walsh for working with some of these materials in their classes and sharing their experiences—and often the work of their students—with me. I am also grateful to all the students in my Writing 20 courses at Duke with whom I tried out one version or the other of this text and the ideas behind it. I especially thank Lorne Bycoff, Julie Flom, Pureum Kim, Keith Greenberg, Justin Lee, and Abhijit Mehta—who read parts of the book and reassured me that it felt like the work we had done together in class. And I owe a special debt to Charles Jordan, Justin Lee, Abhijit Mehta, and Emily Murphy for allowing me to quote from their writing in chapter 5.

I've shared ideas and strategies from this book with faculty in workshops at the University of Michigan, Haverford College, North Carolina State University, and the University of Southern Maine—and in each case came out of the room having learned more than anyone else in it. An exceptional set of written reviews from colleagues at other universities also helped me revise and fine-tune the final form of this book. I owe deep thanks to Tom Deans, Virginia Draper, Eli Goldblatt, Anne Jurecic, Michael Hennessy, Carol Rutz, and Raul Sanchez for their close and sympathetically critical comments on my work. I found their remarks more genuinely useful than any other reviews I have had of my writing.

My thanks also go to those friends who read various parts of this manuscript as I was working on it and whose responses helped keep me going. Nancy Koerbel, Frank Lehner, Kate Harris, and Tina Bessias made me feel at an early point in my writing that I might actually have something to say. Mike Rose offered astute and supportive thoughts both as I began work on this project and as I was finishing it. And David Kaufer and Joe Janangelo each took generous amounts of time to make detailed and perspicacious comments on an early draft of my full text. I was also prodded along gently by my friend Pakis Bessias, who at the start of each of our Sunday morning runs would ask me how much I had written the week before, and then congratulate me on whatever my answer was.

I was saddened while at work on this book by the loss of two people very close and dear to me—my mother, Doreen Harris, and my father-in-law, Jose Vilanova. I miss them both deeply. But I was buoyed, as always, by the warmth, laughter, affectionate irreverence, and good company of my wife, Patricia, and my daughters, Kate and Mora. The last book was for Pat, this one is for the girls.

—jh
Durham, April 2006

Index

abstract, précis, 20, 32, 85, 94, 108, 110, 112–14, 120

acknowledgments, 94, 96, 138

adversarial argument, pro-con debate, 6, 26–27, 36, 58, 63, 72, 117

agonism, 43, 57, 63, 68, 128

allusions, 32

arguing the other side, 48, 58–59, 61, 68

Aristotle, 22–23

Austin, J. L., 3–4

authorizing, 40, 45–46, 50, 88

Barthes, Roland, 1, 46–49, 53, 130

Bartholomae, David, 36, 138

Bell, Thomas, 117–18

Berger, John, 59–61, 63–64, 68, 70, 75, 78, 92, 97

Bettelheim, Bruno, 90–91

bias, 22, 87, 89

block quotes, 30–32, 74, 97, 104

Booth, Wayne, 66, 68

Borges, Jorge Luis, 14–16

borrowing, 40, 46–52, 62, 76

Braverman, Harry, 87–90, 94

Brown, John Seely, 27, 129

Burke, Kenneth, 35, 37

Calvino, Italo, 130

Carroll, Lewis, 14

civility, 37, 57–58, 68–69, 71–72, 129

Clark, Kenneth, 59–61, 63–64, 70

Cliff, Jimmy, 127

Coles, Robert, 17–18, 26

coming to terms, 4–7, 10, 14–17, 25–29, 33–34, 39, 65, 68, 71, 74, 80, 85, 91, 100, 111, 114, 130

conversation, writing as, 4, 17, 35–39, 47, 57, 105, 124

countering, 4–8, 15, 23, 26, 28, 33, 39, 50, 53, 55–59, 61–65, 68–74, 78, 80, 85, 100, 113–14, 117, 119, 130, 132

Culler, Jonathan, 1

Dewey, John, 84–86

dissenting, 58, 65, 68, 93–94

documenting sources, 2, 9, 29, 45

Doyle, Roddy, 79

drafting, 8, 33, 95, 101–2, 112–13, 125–26

Duguid, Paul, 27, 129

editing, 3, 8, 40, 95–96, 100–113, 115, 125, 134, 136

Ehrenreich, Barbara, 50–52, 92–94, 129, 131

Elbow, Peter, 7

email, 6, 37–38, 40, 47
epigraphs, 31–32
extending, 19, 40, 48–50, 52, 62,
    123

Flower, Linda, 111
forwarding, 4–8, 26, 33, 35, 38–39,
    44–46, 49–53, 57–58, 74, 78, 80,
    100, 115, 132
Foucault, Michel, 81–83
Freud, Sigmund, 18–21, 23, 25, 64,
    90–91

Garber, Marjorie, 49–50, 52, 65
Gilligan, Carol, 18–21, 23, 25, 64
Gitlin, Todd, 41–44, 50, 64
global and local, 20, 104–6, 109–10,
    112, 136–37
Goodwin, Doris Kearns, 88–90, 94
Graff, Gerald, 72

Height, Dorothy I., 24–25, 32
Hitchens, Christopher, 93–95
Holland, Dozier, 74
Holmes, Oliver Wendell, 84–85

illustrating, 40, 50
intellectual, 2–5, 7, 9–10, 21, 26, 29,
    36, 40, 45, 47, 51–52, 54, 56–57,
    63, 66–70, 72–73, 75, 78–80,
    82–86, 89, 91–97, 106, 124, 131,
    133, 135
intertexts, 1, 3–4, 7, 10–11, 15, 17,
    19, 22, 24, 27, 30, 35–37, 41,
    43–46, 48–49, 51, 59, 61, 66, 69,
    71, 75, 77–79, 82, 85, 87, 89–90,
    92, 94, 102, 108, 111, 116, 118,
    121, 123, 129
intertextuality, 2

in-text quotes, 29, 31–32
invention, 73, 102

James, William, 84–85
Jones, Mick, 127
Jordan, Charles, 117, 138

keywords, 17, 20, 40, 79,
King, Stephen, 102–3, 112, 118

Lakoff, George, 129–30
Lanham, Richard, 8
Lee, Justin, 121, 138
Lennon and McCartney, 56
log, writer's, 95

mapping an approach, 34, 92, 97,
    106, 108–10, 116, 120, 126
Marc, David, 48–50, 52–53
Martin, Valerie, 76–77
McCracken, Ellen, 61–62
media, non-print, 42–43, 53–54
Mehta, Abhijit, 107, 138
Menand, Louis, 84–86, 94
metatext, 91–92, 120–21
Millar, Melanie Stewart, 61–63, 65
Monty Python, 56
moves, writerly, 5, 85, 132
Murphy, Emily, 123, 139
Murray, Donald, 7

Nehamas, Alexander, 66–68, 72, 75
neologisms, 41, 90

Ong, Walter, 35

paraphrase, 5, 16, 22, 25, 31
Pattison, Robert, 44
Pears, Iain, 14

Phaedrus, 35, 129
Pierce, C.S., 84–85
"Pierre Menard, the Author of the Quixote," 14–15
Plato, 20, 22–23, 35, 37–38, 48, 129, 131
positive opposing terms, 26, 68
Postman, Neil, 46–48, 50, 66
practice, social, 3, 124
pragmatism, 84–86, 94
projects, 5, 10, 12, 15, 24, 28, 33, 39, 45, 53, 57, 60, 62–63, 72, 76–77, 85, 95, 97, 104, 113, 120, 125, 135
proofreading, 3, 96, 101, 104–5, 109–10, 115, 134, 136
public, 10, 24, 31, 38, 82, 88–89, 105, 131, 136

quotation, 1–2, 16, 21–26, 29–33

reflecting on revision, 106, 109, 115–16
responding towards revision, 105, 136–37
reviews, reviewing, 17, 28–29, 139
revising, 4, 7–9, 34, 38–39, 74, 95, 98–117, 119, 121, 124–26, 134
revising plans, 113–14, 125
Rhys, Jean, 76–77

scare quotes, 31–32, 93
Scribner, Sylvia, 3
Sennett, Richard, 81–84, 94
Sexton, Anne, 77, 130
Shakespeare, 6, 37, 74, 76
shorthand and short-changed, 17–18

sponsoring revision, 132–34
Springsteen, Bruce, 99
Steinem, Gloria, 45
Stone, I. F., 22–23, 129, 131
Strummer, Joe, 127
style, 7–8, 12, 29–30, 42, 51–53, 72, 76, 78–83, 96–97, 100, 104–5, 133, 136
summary, 15–16, 24–25, 68, 91, 113

taking an approach, 4, 7, 53, 74–75, 78, 94, 96, 100
Tannen, Deborah, 72
teaching rewriting, choosing readings, 9, 127
terms of art, 29, 32, 59–60
tracking revision, 106–7, 114
transforming, in academic writing, in fiction and film, in music, 26, 43, 75, 77, 80, 86, 95, 121
translating a text into your own terms, 5, 16, 24, 33, 42, 90
Truffaut, Francois, 44
turning an approach on itself, 80, 84

uncovering values, 58, 61, 64, 68
uses and limits, 17, 26, 28, 33

West, Cornel, 23–25, 31–32, 77, 129
Whitehead, Alfred North, 22
Williams, Joseph, 8
Williams, Raymond, 11, 79, 129
Williams, William Carlos, 17
writer-based prose, 111–12

yes, but . . ., 7, 57

J oseph Harris directs the independent and multidisciplinary Duke University Writing Program. At Duke, he also teaches courses in academic writing, critical reading, writing and social class, images of teaching in fiction and film, and writing pedagogies. His previous books are *A Teaching Subject: Composition Since 1966* and *Media Journal: Reading and Writing about Popular Culture.* From 1994–99, Harris edited *CCC: College Composition and Communication.*